PYTHON PROGRAMMING

The Crash Course for Absolute Beginners - Master the Art of Python Coding for Machine Learning, Data Science & Artificial Intelligence with this Step by Step Guide + Exercises

Mike Cowley

The data contained herein is exclusively and universally available for data purposes. The data is presented without agreement or guarantee of any kind.

TABLE OF CONTENTS

INTRODUCTION

In the early 1980s, Python was designed. Initially, Python did not make its mark in the industry as intended due to the absence of adequate marketing. It also had some inbuilt problems relating to the key idea, which worked as an obstacle in its successful route. With renovation by Google within the twentieth century, improvements were seen in Python, as some needed modifications where made in its set-up and settings. As a consequence, it has acquired the authority and efficiency within itself. Google altered the language's key logic and also removed all of the library's repeated modules and techniques to make it smoother and lighter. Its efficiency has now improved more than three times than before. It, therefore, becomes one of the industry's most powerful languages, gaining tremendous popularity among developers and tech experts over the past decade, turning out to be a gem in the IT industry.

Python is a language of programming that is dynamic and object-oriented and is commonly used to develop web applications. Due to its simplicity, reliability, and simple interface, 90 percent of individuals prefer Python to other technology. It provides strong scripting as well as quick application process development across a wide spectrum of areas. Python promotes, as the basis of several open-source systems, instruments that assist in constructing apps with outstanding levels of safety and efficiency. Python follows procedural and object-oriented coding paradigms, making it simple to preserve the diverse apps written in Python.

Today, many programming languages exist. Some are being used, and some are now deemed outdated. The programming situation has altered dramatically over the past few years as designers and programmers are looking for more universal and accessible languages, and this is why the language of Python has lately become so popular. The Python community is increasing day by day, as many programmers find it one of the most user-friendly programming languages.

Python can run on nearly all Windows, Linux, UNIX, OS/2, Mac, and Amiga operating systems. The dedicated Python development team has written several Python programming language-based applications. It has been used by several businesses, such as Google, Yahoo, and IBM, as a fun and dynamic language. It is also used for writing custom tools, and scripts for unique apps is also commonly used.

C / ObjC / Java / Fortran can be readily interfaced with Python. Python's main characteristics are its natural expression of procedural code, sound introspection skills, high accuracy rate, readable syntax, instinctive object orientation, dynamic data types, readily written extensions and modules in C/C++, comprehensive standard libraries and complete modularity, exceptionally error-based processing, and embeddable as a scripting interface within apps. It also promotes the Internet Communications Engine (ICE) and several other techniques for inclusion.

Python is finding comprehensive use by Python Development Services suppliers worldwide, as a vibrant, general-purpose programming language to develop a wide variety of software applications. It enables designers to use less and readable code to convey the idea. It allows developers to integrate Python with other well-known programming languages and instruments flawlessly.

Python designers often need to use a variety of frameworks and instruments to produce high-end software applications in a short time. These designers are building advanced apps with minimal time and effort, with the assistance of the resources provided by the diverse Python frameworks. Python designers also have the choice to pick from a variety of Python frameworks such as Kivy, Qt, PyGUI, WxPython, Django, Flask, Pyramid, etc., based on the nature and conditions of individual application construction projects. Python is also widely used in the creation of web applications such as Django, Pylons, Image Applications, Software Development, Network Programming, Mobile Applications, Audio / Video Applications, as well as Games Applications such as Eve Online.

Despite what assembly code and C coders might tell us, high-level languages have their place in the toolbox of each programmer, and some of them are much more than a curiosity about computer science. Python, out of the many high-level languages that we can choose from today, seems to be the most interesting for those who want to learn something fresh and remain marketable in the industry. Its no-nonsense implementation of object-oriented programming and its clean and easy-to-understand syntax, make it a language that is fun to learn and use, which can't be said about most other languages.

Python's development today involves different individuals with a broad spectrum of backgrounds, ages and instructional levels - whether you're a student, a computer designer, a housewife, or a retiree, you can be a part of the process. There are always some thorough guidelines to make your introduction to the subject easier and more sustainable to ensure your success. Much guidance can be found on the Internet. However, you can get to know some starting points and steps of the method here.

In this *Python Programming*eBook, you will also learn how to write apps using command-line alternatives, read and write to pipes, access variables in the setting, manage interrupts, read and write to documents, generate temporary files, and also write to system logs. In other words, instead of the ancient boring "Hello World," you will discover recipes to write true apps. That is truly awesome stuff!

CHAPTER ONE

PROGRAMMING LANGUAGES

A program is simply a series of instructions that tell a computer what to do. A language a computer can comprehend. However, we are the ones who need to provide those directions. It would be great if, like in science fiction films, we could tell a computer what to do using our native language. Unfortunately, despite the ongoing attempts of many top-flight computer scientists (including your author), designing a computer to comprehend human language is still an unresolved problem.

Even if machines could comprehend us, it is not very suitable for human languages to describe complicated algorithms. Ambiguity and imprecision are fraught with natural language. If I say, for instance, "I saw the guy with the telescope in the park," did I have the telescope, or did the guy? And who's been in the park? Only because all beings share a vast store of common knowledge and experience, do we most times understand messages conveyed. Even so, miscommunication is still widespread.

Computer scientists have tackled this issue by developing notes for the precise and unambiguous manner of expressing computations. These unique notes are called the languages of programming. Each structure has a precise form (its syntax) and a precise meaning (its semantics) in a programming language. A programming language is something like a code that enables a computer to write down the directions.

A variety of languages are accessible and appropriate for web programming. There is no reason to think that any language will prevail entirely and monopolize the scene of web programming. When creating a straightforward website, the issue of which programming language and framework to choose from may arise for items like contact submission forms, picture galleries, jQuery slider, or any other dynamic content elements that the webserver generates. When looking for a web designer or web developer, you'll hear them say, "We're programming in PHP" or "We're developing in ASP.NET / C #." You may wonder what they're talking about and who will provide the best service.

As you can see, web developers can choose to create their web applications with a relatively nice choice of languages. There are many more languages accessible, some more specific than others; for example, VRML. For at least a few of the frameworks, most designers have a working understanding but tend to specialize in one. New languages and language extensions are being created to enhance the daily usability of the Internet. Here we'll look at some of the important languages that over the years have shaped the Internet as well as give a brief overview of each.

Python PHP C JAVA language is one of the programming languages being used today. Python's many advantages make it different from others. Its apps have made it a required language for the creation of software, web development, graphic design, and other usage instances. Its standard libraries support internet protocols like HTML, JSON, XML, IMAP, FTP, etc., and they can also support numerous activities such as data scraping, NLP and other machine learning apps. Students prefer Python programming tutorial rather than other languages due to such benefits and numerous opportunities for utilization. The many internet video coaching courses about Python, which are easily accessible and can be purchased from anywhere by users or any interested candidates, make it more appealingPython programming can be learned in the comfort of your own home.

In reality, programmers often refer to their programs as computer code, and coding is called the process of composing an algorithm in a language of programming. Python is one example of a language of programming. It's the language we're going to use throughout this book. There are other languages, like C++, Java, Perl, Scheme, or BASIC. While in many details these languages differ, they all share the property of having well-defined and unambiguous syntax and semantics. All of the languages mentioned above are examples of computer languages at the highest level. They are intended to be used and understood by humans, even though they are more accurate or precise than the language we use. Strictly speaking, only a very low-level language known as a machine language can be understood by computer hardware.

If we wanted to add two digits to the computer, the instructions performed by the CPU maybe something like this:

1. Load the number from the 2001 memory location into the CPU
2. Load the number from the 2002 memory location into the CPU
3. Add the two numbers in the CPUs
4. Store the result to the location 2003

This seems like a lot of work to add two numbers. It is even more complex than this because, in binary notation, the instructions and numbers are depicted as sequences of 0s and 1s.

The addition of two numbers can be conveyed more naturally in a high-level language such as Python: c= a+ b. This seems easy for humans to understand, but we need some way to translate the high-level language into the language of the machine so that the computer can perform. There are two methods to do this. These are compiling or interpreting a high-level language.

A compiler is a complicated computer program that takes another program written in a high-level language and translates it into some computer's machine language, and then into an equivalent program. The program at the high level is called *source code*, and the resulting machine code is a program that the computer can execute directly.

An interpreter is a program that simulates a high-level linguistic computer. Rather than translating the source program into an equivalent machine language, the interpreter will analyze and execute instructions for the source code.

The distinction between interpreting and compiling is that compiling is a one-shot translation; once a program is compiled, the compiler or source code may run over and over again. For interpretation, each time the program runs, the interpreter and the source are required. Because the translation is performed once and for all, compiled programs tend to be quicker, but interpreted languages lend themselves to a more flexible programming environment as programs can be created and interactively run.

Another benefit that high-level languages have over machine language is highlighted by the translation method called portability. The particular CPU's designers create a computer's machine language.

WHY PYTHON LEARNING?

High-level programming languages such as C, C++, and Java are easily available. The excellent news is that all programming languages of a high standard are very comparable to each other. The main differences are the syntax, the accessible libraries and how we access these libraries. A library is just a collection of resources and pre-written codes we can use when writing our programs. If you are learning a language well, in a fraction of the time it took you to learn the first language; you can easily learn a new language. Therefore, Python is a good place to begin if you're new to programming. Python's simplicity is one of the main characteristics that makes it the ideal language for beginners to learn. Most Python programs involve significantly fewer lines of code, compared to other languages such as C, to perform the same job. This results in fewer programming mistakes and decreases the time required for growth.

Furthermore, Python comes with a comprehensive set of resources from third parties that extend the language's capacities. Python can, therefore, be used for a wide range of functions, including desktop applications, database applications, network programming, game programming, and even mobile development. Last but not least, Python is a cross-platform language, meaning that code written for an operating system like Windows will work well on Mac OS or Linux without making any changes to the Python code.

Python features

Why is machine learning using Python preferable to other languages? This is because, unlike other programming languages, Python has some unique characteristics. Python's fundamental characteristics, which makes it better than other languages, are based on Python's high-level language. It implies Python's context is more user-friendly than the language of the computer.

Python developers can create effective and strong internet apps

Python developers can create high-performance business-standard software applications in separate domains due to their tremendous strength and effectiveness. Python's tag line is "batteries included," meaning that all the necessary modules, techniques, and courses are inside the language through various libraries. Well, the development method becomes much easier than before because of the existence of all these resources. Also, these built-in resources are extremely optimized and can, therefore, provide better mileage for the Python developer. To add to this, the resources are highly consistent with other language parts, making it even stronger.

Python allows software developers to build contemporary apps in various fields

Since C++ and Java strongly influenced Python, we can expect a lot of its characteristics in Python C++ and Java. Python can create any implementation just like Java, i.e., a Python developer can create desktop software, web application, hardware or even smartphone games. This is truly a great characteristic of Python, and it allows its designers not to restrict their talent in any particular domain. They can create any application regardless of domain, device, and platform.

Reliability and quality are paramount

Python is renowned for its effectiveness, velocity, and reliability. Under any circumstances, you can project a Python application, and you'll get an amazing performance there. It's highly safe and secure, as well. It can use 128bit encryption technology to develop extremely safe business-standard apps. Besides, multi-tier safety measures can be applied in your implementation of Python.

Python's interactive nature makes it easy and user-friendly. Users can inspect the output for each declaration in interactive mode. It enables the reuse and recycling of programs as an object-oriented programming language. Python's syntax can be extended through many libraries.

How to Learn Python

Python has been displayed in its huge apps and uses cases. It is mostly used as a basic programming language in Machine Learning and Artificial Intelligence firms. Students wishing to begin their AI and machine learning careers should have a fundamental knowledge of Python. Also, it's a simple programming language for beginning programmers. It can be taught rapidly, owing to its readable and understandable syntax. We can create anything through computer programs with Python. We only need to spend time understanding Python and its standard libraries. PyCharm is its IDE, which, while learning, makes the interface so simple and comfortable. By using PyCharm's debugging function, we can readily analyze each line's output and readily detect the mistake.

Python is used in many large businesses such as Google, Instagram, Dropbox, Reddit, and many more, which implies the large scope of work that it can be used in. Because of the growing demand for Python programmers, industry learners and beginners choose Python as their key programming language. Python's characteristics also make learning very simple. It can be concluded that Python's strong language for growth is the best language for beginners. It's useful for both numerical and scientific activities. Thus, many learners choose internet python programming tutorial video training classes. So, they can learn from anywhere in Python programming and create their careers.

Python language has become so well-known that every field and industry now uses it. Although the other languages of programming are still being used, Python is increasing its fan base. As a result, more and more individuals now aspire to know Python, making it more appealing for persons to seek certification in Python programming. Here are some reasons discussed below.

Machine learning

Today, almost everything goes through algorithms, whether it is a search engine, social media, chatbots, or virtual assistants such as

Cortana. The outcome of machine learning is based on these advanced algorithms, and it has altered the whole technological situation. The main programming language used with machine learning is Python, and you can find many libraries devoted only to machine learning.

Big data

Python is most used in data science, and it requires knowledge in this programming language from the experts in this sector. Although many other languages are used for data science, Python continues to be the favorite language. This is due to the diversity it enables in automation technology, along with the multiple access system and libraries, such as NumPy, PyBrain, etc.

Web development

A lot of websites are being created using Python language these days, one such being Reddit. The primary reason why web development uses the Python programming language is because of its speed and efficiency. It can take hours to use PHP to develop a website while using Python will take just a few minutes. There are also frameworks and libraries such as Django and Flask which can also perform such tasks.

Readability

Python is intended to work with English, making it simple to read. There are also strict punctuation rules on the program, so you don't just look at brackets everywhere. Python also ensures that thanks to a set of guidelines in place, the programmer understands how to format everything. This makes it simple for everyone to generate a code that others can follow.

Libraries

Python libraries has been around for over 25 years, and since it's one of the simplest codes to learn how to use, a few distinct codes have been written using the scheme. The excellent news is that this scheme is open so that any programmer can use the code. In your system, you can install the Python program and use it for your personal use. Python's library is simple to use, whether you use the codes to complete a product or write some of your codes. The codes you want will be mounted in the libraries, and since the program has been around for a long time, they will cover almost anything – from automating your server to creating photo changes.

Community

Because Python is so popular, its community of users is quite large. There are conferences and workshops available for those interested in these programming products, and many opportunities for networking. Thus, an increase in locations – online and offline – to ask questions or learn more about the program. If you're a beginner with Python, you might want to consider checking out some of these places.

Simple

Let's reiterate for emphasis – Python is a simple language of programming. This is the main reason why many programmers prefer it.It is a user-friendly language for beginners because it does not require any complicated codes and syntaxes that are incomprehensible. Python has an easy-to-read syntax and coding that makes it much easier to set up and use.

Python is one of the best choices you can make if you're interested in getting started with coding. It's easy to get started, and as it's going to work on a multitude of distinct platforms, such as your personal computer. Because it's easy to read, coding doesn't have to be a challenge, and you can build your own or learn from others in no time.

Convinced that Python is THE language to be learned? If your response is a yes, let's begin.

Installing Python

We need to download a suitable interpreter for our PCs before we can write our first Python program.

Go to https:/www.python.org/downloads/ to install the Python interpreter. At the top of the webpage should be shown the right version. Click on Python's recent version and begin downloading the software.

Two factors depend on the installer to use:

1. The Windows, Mac OS, or Linux operating system and 2. The processor you are using (32-bit vs64-bit).

For example, you'll probably use the "Windows x86-64 MSI installer" if you're using a 64-bit Windows computer. To download it, press the connection. If you are downloading and running the incorrect installer, there are no concerns. You will receive an error message, and the interpreter will not install it. Just download the installer that's right, and you're ready to go. You are prepared to start coding in Python once you have effectively installed the interpreter.

COMMON TERMS YOU SHOULD KNOW WITH PYTHON

It's essential to know some of the phrases that can make programming easy to comprehend. These basic terms should be understood before you seek to delve more into Python programming. This section will take some time to look at the distinct phrases that are prevalent in Python programming, especially those you will encounter in this guidebook, which will help you prevent confusion and help you get started with your first application.

Class — this is a template used to create objects that have been defined by the user.

Docstring — this is a string that will appear in a module, feature, or class definition as the first phrase lexically. Documentation tools will have the object available.

Function— this is a code block that is invoked when a calling program is used. It is best used to provide a calculation or an independent service.

IDLE — this represents Python's Integrated Development Environment. This is the fundamental setting for interpreters and editors that you can use together with Python. It's useful for beginners and is very budget-friendly. It is a clear example of code and will not waste much time or space.

Immutable — this is an object assigned a fixed value within the code. Tuples, strings, and numbers could be included. You can't change the object, and you need to produce and first store a fresh item with distinct value. In some instances, this can be useful, for example, the keys in a dictionary.

Interactive — one thing about Python that many beginners like is that it's so interactive. In the interpreter, you can experiment with different things and see the outcomes immediately. It's a nice way to enhance your programming abilities and test your fresh concept.

List— this is a built-in Python datatype. It includes a changing series of sorted values. It can also include unchangeable numerical and string values.

Mutable — these are the objects that can change their value within the program but are capable of maintaining their original ID.

Object — this is any information with a state, such as a value or an attribute, as well as a specified behavior or process within Python. The two primary kinds of Python available are Python 2 and Python 3 (Python 3000). Many individuals have stuck with Python 2 because like using the older version databases, and there are no backward capabilities in Python 3.Python 3000 is a mythical Python alternative that allows you to use it and the Python 2 backward capacity.

String— this is one of Python's most fundamental kinds that will store the text. The strings will store text in Python 2, so that the sort of string can then be used to retain binary data.

Triple cited string— this is a string that has either the single quote or the double quote in three cases. It might be like''' I enjoy tacos'''.These are used for many purposes. They can assist you in a string to have double and single quotes and make it simpler to go over a few lines of code without problems.

Tuple — this is a Python's built-in datatype. This data type is an ordered sequence of values that cannot be changed. The sequence is the only unchangeable component. It may involve some mutable values, such as getting inside a dictionary where the values may alter.

Type — this is a category or kind of information represented in the languages of the programming. These kinds will vary in their characteristics as well as in their features and techniques, including immutable and mutable alternatives. Python involves some kinds of dictionaries: tuple, list, floating-point, long, integer, and string.

PYTHON'S MAGIC

Now that you have all the technical information, it's time for you to have fun with Python. The ultimate objective is to create our bidding on the computer. To this end, we are going to write programs that regulate the machine's computational procedures. You will soon realize that there's not much magic in this phase, but programming may feel like magic in some respects.

Inside the computer, the computing procedures are like magical spirits we can harness for our job. These spirits, unfortunately, only understand a very arcane language we don't know. In extending this analogy, what we need is a sympathetic genie who can guide the spirits in fulfilling our desires. Our genie is an interpreter from Python. We can offer the Python interpreter directions and direct the underlying spirits to fulfill our requirements.

In a unique language of spells and incantations (i.e., Python), we interact with the genie. The best way to begin learning about Python is by letting our genie out of the bottle and trying some spells.

In an interactive mode, you can begin the Python interpreter and type in some instructions to see what is going on. You may see something like:

Python 2.1 (# 1, June 21, 2001, 11:39:00)

[GCCpgc-2.91.66 19990314 (egcs-1.1.2 release)] on linux2

"copyright" type, "credits" or "permit" for more data when you begin the interpreter program first.

>>>

The >>> is a Python prompt that tells us that genie is waiting for us to give it a command. A full command is called a **statement** in programming languages.

Here's a Python interpreter sample communication.

>>> print "Hello, Universe"

 Hello, World

>>> Print 2 + 3

5 >>> Print "2 + 3=," 2 + 3

 2 + 3= 5

I used the Python print statement to try out three examples. The first declaration asks Python to show 'Hello world,' the literal sentence. Python replies by printing the phrase on the next line. Python is asked by the second print statement to print the sum of 2 and 3. These two concepts are combined in the third print.

Python prints the portion in "2+ 3=" quotes, followed by adding 2 + 3, which is 5.

This type of interaction is a wonderful way for Python to try fresh stuff. This book is sprinkled with snippets of interactive sessions. If you see the Python prompt in an example, you should be advised to illustrate an interactive session. Fire Python up and try the examples for yourself.

We usually want to move beyond snippets and perform a whole series of statements. Python allows us to put together a series of statements to produce a brand-new command called a function. Here is an instance of a fresh feature called 'hello' being created.

```
>>> def hello():
        print "Hello."
        print, "Computers are fun."
        >>>
```

The first line informs Python that a fresh feature called hello is being defined. To demonstrate that they are components of the 'hello' feature, the following lines are indented. The blank line (pressing the < Enter > button twice) allows Python to understand that the definition is completed, and the interpreter will respond with a different prompt.

Note that nothing was happening in the definition. We told Python what should happen when using the hello function as a command; we didn't ask Python to do it yet.

By typing your name, a function is invoked. When we use our hello command, this is what happens.

```
>>> Hello ()

Hello

>>>
```

Do you see what this is all about? The two hello function print statements are performed in sequence.

In defining and using hello, you may be wondering about the parentheses. Commands can have changing components called parameters inside the parentheses. Let's take a look at a custom greeting instance using a parameter. First, the definition:

```
>>> def greet(someone):

        print "Hello," somebody

        prints. "How are you?"
```

We can now use our personalized greeting.

```
>>> greet ("Sam)
Hello Sam
How are you?
Hello Helen
>>> greet("Helen)
```

Hello Helen

How are you?
>>>

Could you see what's going on here? We can submit distinct names when we use 'greet' to customize the outcome. We will discuss the parameters later in detail. For the time being, our functions will not use parameters so that the parentheses will be empty, but when defining and using functions, you still need to include them.

One issue with interactively entering features at the Python prompt like this, is that when we leave Python, the definitions go away. We have to write them all over again if we want to use them the next time. Usually, programs are developed by typing definitions into a distinct module or script file. This file is stored on a disk to allow it to be used again and again.

A module file is just a text file, and you can generate one using any text editing program, such as a notepad or word processor (if you save your program as a "simple text" file). The process is simplified by a unique program type known as a programming environment. Specifically intended to assist programmers, a programming environment involves characteristics such as automatic indenting, color emphasis, and interactive development. The standard distribution of Python includes a programming environment called *Idle,* which can be used in this book to work on the programs.

Let's demonstrate the use of a module file by writing a full program and running it. Our program will demonstrate a notion known as chaos in mathematics. Here's the program we'd like to type it into Idle or some other editor, and save it to a module file:

```
# File: chaos.py
# A simple program is illustrating chaotic behavior.
def main():
print "This program illustrates a chaotic function."
x = input("Enter a number between 0 and 1: ")
for I in range(10):
x = 3.9 * x * (1 - x)
print x
main()
```

This file should be saved with the name chaos.py. The.py extension shows that this is a module for Python. You can see that there are lines in this particular example to define a new function called main.

Programs are often placed in the main function. The last line of the file is the invoke function command. Don't worry if you don't know what the main is doing; in the next chapter, we'll address it. The point here is that we can run it whenever we want when we have a program in a module file.

This program can be operated in various ways depending on the real operating system and programming environment you are using. You can run a Python program by double-clicking on the icon of the module file if you are using a windowing system. You could type a command like python chaos.py in a command-line scenario. If you use Idle (or other programming environments) you can run a program by opening it in the editor and then selecting a command such as import or execute.

Starting the Python interpreter and then importing the file, is one technique that should always operate. This is how it looks.

```
>>> Import chaos

This program shows a chaotic function

Enter the number between 0 and 1:.25
0.73125
0.76644140625
 0.698135010439
0.82189581879
 0.570894019197
0.95398748364
0.166186721954
0.540417912062
 0.9686289303
0.1185090176
>>>
```

Entering the first line import chaos tells the Python interpreter to load the chaos module from the file chaos.py to the main memory. Note that on the import line, I did not include the.py extension. Python assumes that the module will have an extension of.py.

As the module file is imported by Python, each line is executed. It's just like at the interactive Python prompt; we typed them one-by-one. The module default causes the main function to be created by Python. When the last line of the module is met by Python, the main function is invoked, and our program runs. The running program asks the user to enter a number between 0 and 1 (I typed ".25" in this situation) and then to print a sequence of 10 digits.

Python generates a companion file with a.pyc extension when you first import a module file this way. Python than produces a different file on the disk called chaos.pyc in this instance. This is a Python interpreter's intermediate file. Technically, a hybrid compilation /interpretation process is used by Python. The source of Python in the module file is compiled into more primitive byte code instructions. It then interprets this byte code (the.pyc) file. The second time that a.pyc file is accessible makes the importation of a module quicker. However, if you want to save the disk room, you can delete the byte code files; as required, Python will automatically re-create them.

Only once a module has to be imported into a meeting. We can run the program again after loading the module by requesting Python to perform the primary command. Using unique dot notation, we do this: Type chaos.main. () Tells Python to invoke the chaos module's primary feature. Continuing with our instance, this is how it looks when we resume running the program as the input with 26.

>>> chaos.main ()

Enter the amount from 0 to 1:.26

0.75036
0.73054749456
0.767706625733
 0.6954993339
0.825942040734
0.560670965721
0.960644232282
0.147446875935
 0.490254549376
0.974629602149
>>>

The output of the chaos program may not look very exciting inside a Python program, but it illustrates a very interesting phenomenon known to physicists and mathematicians. Take a line-by-line look at this program and see what it is doing. Do not worry about understanding every detail immediately. In subsequent chapters, we will return to all these ideas.

The program's first two lines begin with the character #:

#File: chaos.py

#A straightforward program that illustrates chaotic conduct.

These lines are referred to as comments. They are designed for the program's human readers, and Python ignores them. The Python interpreter always skips through the end of a row any text from the pound sign (#).

The program's next line starts to define a function called main:

def main():

Strictly speaking, the primary feature would not have to be created. Since a module's lines are executed as they are loaded, without this definition, we could have written our program. That is, the module might have looked this way:

#File: chaos.py

```
#A simple program that illustrates chaotic behavior.

print "This program shows a messy feature."

x= input ("Enter a number between 0 and 1:")

 for I in range (10):

x= 3.9* x* (1-x)

print  x
```

This version is slightly shorter, but it is usual to put the directions containing the program inside the primary feature. This approach has illustrated an immediate benefit, as seen above. It allows us to (re)run the program by simply invoking chaos.main). To run it again, we do not need to reload the module from the file, which would be necessary in the main-less case. The first line within the main is the start of our program. Print "This program shows a messy function." This line causes Python to print a message that introduces the program when running. Look at the program's next line.x= input ("Enter a number from 0 to 1:"). X is a variable example. A variable is used to give a value a name so that at other points in the program we can refer to it. The whole row is a declaration of the input. When this statement is received by Python, it displays the quoted message "Enter a number between 0 and 1:" and then pauses, waiting for the user to type something on the keyboard and pressing the < Enter > key. The user type value will then be stored as the variable. The user entered.25 in the first instance above, which becomes the value of x.

The following statement is a loop example.

For I in scope (10)

A loop is a tool that tells Python to do the same thing repeatedly. This particular loop tells you to do something 10 times something. The lines indented under the heading of the loop are 10-fold statements. These make up the loop's body.

x= 3.9* x* (1-x)

print x

The loop impact is precisely the same as if we had written the loop body 10 times:

x = 3.9 * x * (1 - x)
print x
x = 3.9 * x * (1 - x)
print x
x = 3.9 * x * (1 - x)
print x
x = 3.9 * x * (1 - x)
print x

```
x = 3.9 * x * (1 - x)
print x
x = 3.9 * x * (1 - x)
print x
x = 3.9 * x * (1 - x)
print x
x = 3.9 * x * (1 - x)
print x
x = 3.9 * x * (1 - x)
print x
x = 3.9 * x * (1 - x)
print x
```

But, what are these statements doing exactly? The first calculation is performed.

$$3.9 * x * (1-x)$$

The assignment statement is called. A mathematical expression is a component on the correct hand of the=. To indicate multiplication, Python uses the* character. Remember that x is 0.25 (from the declaration input). The calculated value is either 3.9(0.25) (1−0.25) or 0.73125. Once the value is calculated on the right side, it will be stored (or assigned) back to the variable that appears on the left side of the=;

in this case, x. The fresh x (0.73125) value replaces the ancient (0.25) value.

The second line in the body of the loop is a kind of declaration we have met before – a declaration of print.

Print x

The current value of x will be displayed on the screen when Python executes this statement. The first output number is 0.73125.

Remember that the loop is running 10 times. After the x value has been printed, the two-loop statements are performed again.

$3.9^* x^* (1-x)$

Print x

Naturally, x now has a value of 0 for 73125, so the equation calculates a fresh value of x as $3.9(0.73125)(1-0.73125)$, which is 0.7664140625.

Can you see how x's current value is used every time around the loop to calculate a new value? That's where the figures came from in the run of the instance. You may attempt to work yourself for a distinct input value through the program steps (say 0.5), then use Python to operate the program and see how well a computer has been impersonated.

EXERCISE

1. List and describe the advantages of python programming in your own words and clarify why you are learning python.

2. List the Python programming popular terms

3. As you will find out in a subsequent section, many of the figures stored on a computer are not accurate values, but close approximations. The value 0.1, for instance, could be stored as 0.1000000000000000555. Usually such tiny distinctions are not an issue; however, considering what you learned about chaotic behavior in the previous section, in certain situations, you should understand the need for caution. Can you think of examples where this could be an issue? Explain each.

4. Use 0.15 as the input value to trace the Chaos program by the side. Show the resulting output sequence.

5. Using whatever Python application you have available, enter and operate the Chaos program used as an instance. Try it with different input values to see how it works, as described in the chapter.

6. Modify the Chaos program by using 2.0 instead of 3.9 as the logistics function multiplier. Your modified code row should look like this:x= 2.0 * x* (1-x). Run the program for different input values and compare the outcomes with the initial program outcomes. Write a brief

paragraph that describes any differences you notice in the two versions' behavior.

7. Change the Chaos program so that 20 values are printed instead of 10.

CHAPTER TWO

THE WORLD OF VARIABLES AND OPERATORS

You will learn everything about variables and operators in this chapter. In particular, you will understand what variables are and how they can be named and declared. We're also going to look at the common activities we can do on them. Ready? Let's get going.

What variables are there?

Variables are names provided in our programs for information that we need to store and manipulate. For example, assume that your program needs to store a user's age. To do this, we can use the following statement to name this data: userAge. We then define the userAge variable.

UserAge=0

Your program will allocate a certain area of your computer's storage space to store this data after you define the userAge variable. By referring to it by its name, userAge, you can then access and modify this data. You must give it an initial value each time you declare a new variable. We've given it the value0 in this example. In our program, we can always alter this value later.

We can identify various variables in one go, as well. Simply write userAge, userName= 30,' David '

This is equivalent to

userAge= 30

userName=' David '

Naming a variable

A letter in Python can contain only letters (a-z, A-B), numbers or underscores. However, a number cannot be the first character. You can, therefore, name your userName, user name or userName2 variables, but not 2userName.

Furthermore, there are some reserved words that you cannot use as a variable name because they already have pre-assigned Python meanings. These words reserved include phrases such as printing, input, if, while, etc. In the following chapters, we will learn about each of them.

Finally, the names of the variable are sensitive to cases. UserName is not identical to userName.

When naming a variable in Python, there are two conventions. We can use either the notation of the camel case or the underscores. Camel's case is the practice of writing mixed-casing compound words (e.g., thisIsAVariableName). This is the convention we're going to use in the remainder of the text. Alternatively, use underscores to divide phrases is another prevalent practice. You can name your variables such as this if you prefer: this is a variable name.

The Assignment Sign

Note that the= sign in the userAge= o declarations, has a distinct significance from the= sign we learned in math. The= sign is recognized as an assignment sign when programming. It implies we assign the value to the variable on the left on the correct side of the= sign. A useful way to comprehend the userAge= o declaration is to consider it as userAge <-o.

Thex= y and y=x statements have very distinct programming meanings.

Confused? This is probable to be clarified by an instance.

Enter and save the following code in your Idle editor.

x = 5

y= 10

x= y

print('x=', x)

print(' y=', y)

Now run. This output should be obtained:

x= 10

y= 10

While x has an original value of 5 (stated in the first row), in the third, rowx= y gives the value of y to x(x <-y), thus altering the value fromx to 10 while the value of y stays unchanged.

Next, change the program by changing ONLY ONE statement: from x= y to y= x. Change the third line. Mathematically, it implies the same thing x= y and y= x. This is not the case in programming, though.

Run the second schedule. You are now going to get

x= 5

y= 5

You can see that the x value stays as 5 in this instance, but the y value is shifted to 5. This is because the y=x declaration assigns x to y (y <-x) value. Y will be 5, while x will be unchanged as 5.

Basic Operators

We can also conduct the usual mathematical operations on variables in addition to assigning an original value to a variable. Basic operators in Python include:

+ (addition): Adds values on either side of the operator.

- (sottraction): Subtracts right-hand operand from the left-hand operand.

49

* (Multiplication): Multiplies values on either side of the operator

/ (division): Divides left-hand operand by right-hand operand

% (Modulus): Divides left-hand operand by right-hand operand and returns remainder

** (exponent): Performs exponential (power) calculation on operators

// (floor division): rounds the response to the closest whole number

Examples:

Addition: x + y= 7

Subtraction: x - y= 3

Multiplication: x * y= 10

Division:x / y= 2.5

Floor Division: x/y= 2 (rounds the response to the closest whole number)

Modulus: x % y= 1 (provides the rest when 5 is split by 2)

Exponent: x**y= 25 (5 at 2)

More Assignment Operators

In addition to the= sign, there are a few more assignment operators. In the example: Suppose x= 5, y= 2 Addition:x + y= 7 Subtraction:. These include +=, -= and*= operators.

Suppose we've got the x variable with an original 10 value. If we want to increase x by 2, we can write x= x+ 2. The program will first assess the correct(x+ 2) phrase and assign the response to the left. Thus, the above declaration ultimately becomes x <-12.

Instead of writing x=x+ 2to express the same significance, we can also write x+= 2. In fact, the+= sign is a shorthand combining the assignment sign with the addition operator. Therefore, x+= 2 implies merelyx=x+ 2.

Likewise, we can write x= x-2 or x-= 2 if we want to do subtraction. The same operates for all the seven carriers listed in the above section.

Exercise:

1. What are the variables?

2. Example the use of various variables

3. List the core operators

CHAPTER THREE

PYTHON DATA TYPES

In this chapter, we will first look at some fundamental Python data types, namely integer, float, and string. Next, we will investigate the casting type concept. Finally, in Python, we're going to discuss three more sophisticated information kinds – the list, tuple, and dictionary.

Integers

Integers are numbers that do not have decimal components, such as-5, -4, -3, 0, 5, 7 etc. Simply write variableName= initial value, to declare an integer in Python. Example:

userAge= 20, mobileNumber= 12398724

Float

Float refers to numbers with decimal parts like 1.234, -0.023,12.01. We write variableName= original value

Example: userHeight= 1.82, userWeight= 67.2

String Data Type

A string is a series of characters to declare a float in Python. Python also enables single quotes (apostrophes) to delimit strings. There's no difference— just use a corresponding set for sure. Strings, like numbers, can be stored in variables. Here are some instances of these two literal string types.

```
>>> str1= "Hello"

>>> str2=' spam'

>>> print str1, str2

Hello spam

>>>type(str1)

<type' string'

>>>type(str2)

<type' string'>
```

Some programs also require the user to receive string input (e.g., a name). It takes a lot of care to get string-valued input. Remember that the declaration of input serves as an expression to be assessed, whatever the customer types. Consider the interaction below.

```
>>> Input= first name ("Please enter your name:")

Please enter your name: Sam

Traceback (innermost last):

"< pyshell#8 >" file, row 1, in?
```

FirstName= input ("Type in your name:")

"< string >" file, line 0, in?

NameError:Sam

There's something wrong here. Can you see the issue?

Remember, only a delayed expression is an input declaration. When I entered the name "Sam," this had the same effect as executing this assignment statement: firstName= Sam. This statement says, "look up the value of the John variable and store that value in firstName." Since Sam was never given a value, Python could not find any variable with that name and respond with a NameError. One way to solve this issue is to type citations around a string input to evaluate it as a literal string.

>>> FirstName= input ("Please enter your name:")

Please enter your name: "Sam."

>>> "Hello" print, firstName

Hello Sam

This works, but it's not a very good solution. We should not have to burden our program users with details such as typing quotes around their names. Python has a better system. The raw input feature is the same as the input function except that it does not assess the user type expression. The input is transmitted as a text string to the program.

Here's how it looks with raw input:

>>> firstName= raw input ("Please enter your name:")

Please enter your name: Sam

>>>print "Hello", firstName

Hello Sam

Built-In String Functions

Python involves several built-in string manipulation functions. A feature is merely a reusable code block that performs a specific job. The upper technique for strings is an instance of a feature accessible in Python. You use it in a string to capitalize on all the letters. For example,' Peter.' upper, gives us the "PETER" string.

It is also possible to format strings using the percentage of Operator Strings that are using the percent operator. This provides you more control over how to display and store your string. The percentage operator syntax is "string to be formatted" percentage (values or variables to be inserted into a string, divided by commas).

This syntax has three components. First, we write the string in quotes to be formatted. Next, we write the symbol for the percentage. Finally, we have a couple of round brackets () in which we write in the string (the values or variables to be inserted). This round bracket with inside values is effectively known as a tuple, a sort of information that we will discuss later in the section.

Type and execute the following code in IDLE.

Brand=' Apple'

exchangeRate= 1.235235245

message=' This percentage of a laptop is in percentage USD and the exchange rate is in percentage 4.2f USD to 1 EUR' full (brand,1299, exchangeRate) print (message)

In the above instance, the string 'This percentage of a laptop is in percentage USD, and the "exchange rate is in percentage 4.2f USD to 1 EUR' is the string we want to format. As placeholders in the string, we use the percentages – percentage d and percentage 4.2f formatters.

As indicated in the round brackets, these placeholders will be replaced by the variable brand – the value 1299 and the variable exchange rate, respectively. If we run the code, the output will be displayed below.

The price of this Apple laptop is USD 1299, and the exchange rate is USD 1.24 to EUR 1 The percentage s formatter is used to represent a string ("Apple" in this case), whereas the percentage d formatter is an integer (1299). If we want to add spaces before an integer, to indicate the desired length of the string, we can add a number between percent and d. For example, "percent 5d" percent (123) will give us "123" (with 2 front spaces and a total length of 5).

The f-formatter percentage is used to format floats (decimal number). Here we format it as 4.2f percent, with 4 referring to the complete duration and 2 referring to 2 decimal places. If we want to add spaces before the amount, we can format as a percentage of 7.2f, giving us "1.24" (with 2 decimal places, 3 front spaces, and a complete duration of 7). Use the formatting technique to format strings.

Python also offers us with the formatting technique for formatting strings in addition to using the percent operator for formatting strings. The syntax is "string to format." format (values or variables to be inserted into the string, separated by commas). We do not use percent s, percent for percent d as placeholders when using the formatting technique. Instead, we use curly brackets such as this: message=' The price of this{0:s} laptop is{ 1:d} USD and the exchange rate is{ 2:4.2f} USD to 1 EUR.'.format('Apple', 1299, 1.235235245). Inside the curly bracket, we first write the parameter position to be used, followed by a colon. We write the formater after the colon. Inside the curly brackets, there should be no spaces.

When we write format('Apple', 1299, 1.235235245), the format or technique is passed in three parameters. Parameters are information needed by the technique to accomplish its job. Apple,' 1299 and 1.235235245 are the parameters.

The' Apple' parameter has a position of 0,1299 with a range of 1 and a position of 2.235235245. Positions begin from ZERO at all times.

When we write {0: s}, we ask that the interpreter replace {0: s} with the 0 parameters and that it is a string (because the formatter is).

We refer to the parameter in place 1, which is an integer (formatter is d) when we write {1: d}.

When we write{2:4.2f}, we refer to the float parameter in place 2, which is formatted with 2 decimal locations and a complete duration of 4 (formater is 4.2f).

The cost of this Apple computer is 1299 USD and the exchange rate is 1.24 USD to 1 EUR Note: if you don't want to format the string, you can merely write email=' The price of this{} laptop is{USD} and the exchange rate is {USD to 1 EUR.'.format ('Apple',1299, 1.23523245).

We don't need to indicate the parameter position here. The interpreter replaces the curly brackets based on the order of the given parameters. We'll get this Apple laptop's cost is USD 1299 and the exchange rate is USD 1.235235245 to EUR 1 The format () technique can be confusing for beginners. String formatting may be more fanciful than what we covered here, but for most purposes, what we covered is enough. Try the following program to gain a better knowledge of the format () method.

message1='{0}' is simpler than{1}'.format(' Python," Java')

 message2='{1}' is simpler than{0}'.format(' Python," Java')

message3='{:10.2f}and{: d}'.format(1.234234234, 12)

message4='{}'. format(1.234234234)

print (message1)

 #You'll get' Python is simpler than Java '

print (message2) #You'll get' 1.23 and 12'

#You're going to get 1.234234234.

There's no formatting. You can experiment with the format or technique using the Python Shell. Try typing and see what you get in different strings.

Type Casting in Python

Sometimes we need to convert from one data type to another in our program, such as from an integer to a string. This is called a casting type.

In Python, three built-in functions enable us to cast type. These are the features int, float, and str.

Python's int () feature requires a float or a suitable string and transforms it into an integer. We can write int (5.712987) to switch a float to an integer. As a consequence, we will get 5 (anything after removing the decimal point). We can write int ("4") to modify a string to an integer, and we will get 4. We can't type int ('Hello') or int ('4.22321'), though. In both instances, we will make a mistake.

The float () feature includes an integer or a suitable string and shifts it to afloat. For example, we'll get 2.0 if we type float (2) or float ("2"). If we type float ("2.09109"), we will get 2.09109, which is afloat and not a string since it removes the quotation marks.

On the other hand, the strfunction converts a string to an integer or float. If we type str (2.1), for example, we'll get "2.1."

Now that we addressed Python's three basic types of information and their casting let's move on to the more sophisticated kinds of information.

List

The list relates to a usually associated information collection. We can store this information as a list rather than as distinct variables. For example, assume the age of 5 customers should be stored by our program. It makes more sense to store them as a list instead of storing them as user1Age, user2Age, user3Age, user4Age, and user5Age.

You write listName=[original values] to declare a list. Note that when declaring a list, we use square brackets[]. A comma separates multiple values.

Example:

userAge=[21, 22, 23, 24, 25]

Without assigning any original values, we can also declare a list. We're just writing listName=[]. What we now have is an empty list that contains no items. To add objects to the list, we must use the append () technique listed below.

Individual values are accessible through their indexes in the list, and indexes always start from ZERO, not 1. In almost all programming languages, such as C and Java, this is prevalent practice. The first value, therefore, has an index of 0, the next one has an index of 1 and so on. For example, userAge[0]= 21, userAge [1]= 22

Alternatively, from the back, you can access a list's values. The last item in the list has a-1 index; the last one has a-2 index, and so on. Therefore, [-1] userAge= 25,[-2] userAge= 24.

You can assign a list to a variable, or partthereof. The userAge2 variable becomes[21, 22, 23, 24, 25] if you write userAge2= userAge.

If you write userAge3= userAge [2:4], the list userAge3 will be assigned items with index 2 to index 4-1. UserAge3=[23, 24], in other words.

The 2:4 notations are referred to as a slice. Every time we use Python's slice notation, the item is always included in the start index, but the item at the end is always excluded. Notation 2:4 therefore refers to items from index 2 to index 4-1 (i.e. index3) and therefore userAge3=[23, 24] and not[23, 24, 25].

There is a third number known as the stepper in the slice notation. If we write userAge4= userAge[1:5:2], we will get a sub list of every second amount from index 1 to index 5-1 because the step is 2. UserAge4=[22, 24], therefore.

Furthermore, slice notes have helpful defaults. The default for the first amount is zero, and the volume of the list being sliced is the rule for the second amount. For example, userAge [:4] provides values from index 0 to index 4-1 while userAge [1:] gives values from index 1 to index 5-1 (because userAge is 5, i.e. userAge has 5 items).

We write listName[index of item to be changed]= fresh value to alter items in a list. For example, you write userAge [1] =5 if you want to modify the second item. UserAge=[21, 5, 23, 24, 25] Use the append) (feature to add products. For example, you add the value 99 to the end of the list if you write userAge. Append (99). Your list is now userAge=[21, 5, 23, 24, 25, 99] You write[index of item to be deleted] to delete items. For example, if you write del userAge [2], your list now becomes userAge=[21, 5, 24, 25, 99] (the third item is deleted) Try running the following program to appreciate the workings of a list fully.

#Listing components of different data kinds can be myList=[1, 2, 3, 4, 5, "Hello"] #print the whole list.

[1, 2, 3, 4, 5, "Hello"] #print the third item (recall: index starting from zero).

print (myList[2]) #The last element is 3 #photo.

Print(myList[-1]) #You're going to get "Hello" #assign myList (from index 1 to 4) to myList2 and print myList2 myList2= myList[1:5] print (myList2) #You're going to get[2, 3, 4, 5] #modify the second item in my list and print the updated list myList[1]= 20 print (myList) #You're going to get[1, 20, 3, 4, 5,' Hello'] #Add a fresh item to myList and print the updated list myList.append("How are you) "print

Tuple

Tuples are the same as lists, but their values cannot be modified. The initial values are the remaining values for the rest of the program. An example where tuples are useful is when the names of the months of the year must be stored by your program. You write tupleName= (first values) to declare a tuple.

Note that when we declare a tuple, we use round brackets). A comma separates multiple values.

65

Example: monthsOfYear=(' Jan," Feb," Mar," Apr," May," Jun," Jul," Aug," Sep," Oct," Nov," Dec') Use their indexes to access the individual values of a tuple.

Consequently, monthsOfYear[0]= "Jan"[-1] = "Dec."

Dictionary

Dictionary is an associated PAIRS set of information. For example, we can store them in a dictionary if we want to store the username and age of 5 users.

You write dictionaryName= {dictionary key: information} to declare a dictionary, requiring dictionary keys to be unique (within one dictionary). That is, a dictionary like this myDictionary= {"Peter":38," John":51,"Peter":13} cannot be declared.

This is because twice "Peter" is used as the key for the dictionary. Note that when declaring a dictionary, we use curly brackets{}. A comma separates multiple pairs.

Example: userNameAndAge= {"Peter":38," John":51, "Alex":13," Alvin":"Not Available"}

You may also use dict () to declare a dictionary. To declare the above userNameAndAge dictionary, write userNameAndAge= dict (Peter= 38, John= 51, Alex= 13, Alvin= "Not Available") If you use this technique to declare a dictionary, use round brackets () instead of curly brackets{} and do not place quotation marks on dictionary keys.

We use the dictionary key, which is the first value in the {dictionary key: information} couple, to access individual objects in the dictionary. For example, you write userNameAndAge["John"] to get the age of John.

You're going to get the 51 value.

We write dictionaryName [dictionary key of the object to be altered]= fresh information in order to change objects in a dictionary. For example, we write userNameAndAge ["John"]= 21 to change the "John":51 pair. Now our dictionary is userNameAndAge= {"Peter":38," John":21, "Alex":13,"Alvin":"Not Available"}.

Without assigning any original values, we can also declare a dictionary.

Simply write Name={} dictionary. What we now have is an empty dictionary that contains no objects.

We write dictionaryName [dictionary key]= information for adding objects to a dictionary. For example, we write userNameAndAge["Joe"]= 40, if we want to add" Joe":40 to our dictionary. Our dictionary is now userNameAndAge= {"Peter":38," John":21, "Alex":13," Alvin":"Not Available," "Joe":40} We write del dictionaryName [dictionary key] to extract objects from a dictionary. For example, we write del userNameAndAge["Alex"] to extract the "Alex":13 pair. Our dictionary now becomes userNameAndAge= {"Peter":38," John":21, "Alvin":"Not Available," "Joe":40} Run the program below to see all of these in practice.

#Dictionary, dictionary keys and information can be of distinct information types myDict={' One':1.35, 2.5:'Two Point Five', 3:'+', 7.9:2} #print the entire dictionary print (myDict) #You'll get{ 2.5:' Two Point Five', 3:' +',' One': 1.35, 7.9: 2} #Note that objects in a dictionary are not stored in the same order as you declare them.

#Print key= "One" item.

print (myDict['One'])

 #You're going to get 1.35

#print key= 7.9.

Print (myDict[7.9])

 #You'll get 2

#Modify the item with important= 2.5 and print the updated

myDict dictionary[2.5]= "Two and a Half" print (myDict)

 #You'll get {2.5:' Two and a Half', 3:'+',' One': 1.35, 7.9: 2}

#Add a fresh item and print the updated myDict dictionary[' New item']=' I'm new' print (myDict)

#You'll get {' New item':' I'm new', 2.5:' Two and a Half', 3: '+', 7.9: 2}

Simple String Processing

Our first instance is a computer system username calculation program. Many computer systems use a mixture of usernames and passwords to authenticate users of the scheme. Each user must be assigned a distinctive username by the system administrator. Usernames are often obtained from the real name of the user. One username generation system is to use the first initial of the user, followed by up to seven username letters. Using this technique, Elmer Thudpucker's username would be "ethudpuc," and Sam Smith would be "smith." We want to write a program that reads the name of a person and calculates the username. Our program follows the fundamental pattern of input-process-output. The outcome is as easy as we can skip the creation of the algorithm and jump straight into the code. The algorithm outline is included in the final program as remarks.

```
# username.py
# Simple string processing program to generate usernames.
def main():
print "This program generates computer usernames."
print
# get user's first and last names
first = raw_input("Please enter your first name (all lowercase): ")
last = raw_input("Please enter your last name (all lowercase): ")
# concatenate the first initial with 7 chars of the last name.
uname = first[0] + last[:7]
# output the username
```

```
print "Your username is:," uname
main()
```

First, this program utilizes raw input to get user strings. To produce the username, indexing, slicing and concatenation are then combined.

Here's a run for instance.

This program creates usernames for the computer.

Please enter your first name (all lowercase): Elmer

Please enter your last name (all lowercase): thudpucker

 Your username is: ethudpuc

As you can see, string computing is very comparable to numbers computing.

Here's another issue with string operations that we can fix. Suppose we want to print the month abbreviation corresponding to the amount of a specified month. The program entry is an int representing a monthly amount (1–12), and the output is the acronym for the month in question. For instance, if the input is 3, then for March, the yield should be Mar.

At first, this program might seem to be beyond your present capacity. Experienced programmers acknowledge that this is an issue of choice. That is, we have to decide which output is suitable for 12 distinct inputs, depending on the user's amount. We're not going to cover decision structures until later; however, by some smart use of string slicing, we can write the program now.

The fundamental concept is to store all the names of the month in a large loop.

Months= "JanFebMarAprMayJunJulAugSepOctNovDec" The suitable substring can be searched for a specific month. The trick is where to slice. Since every month is represented by three letters, we could readily extract the abbreviation if we knew where a specified month began in the string.

MonthAbbrev= months[pos: pos+3] This would give us a three-length substring starting in the pos position.

Exercise

You learned the kinds of information and how to generate strings with distinct operators in this chapter. With escape sequences, you saw how to include unique characters in them. You've seen joining and repeating strings. You've learned about python casting and how to work with it. You learned how to work with them about number, integer, float, and how. Therefore, your practice is merely for you to revisit everything you have learned in this section and create yourself some practical examples.

CHAPTER FOUR

FUNCTIONS AND MODULES

We have briefly discussed functions and modules in our past chapters. Let's look into them in detail in this section. To reiterate, all programming languages come with built-in codes that can be used as programmers to make our lives simpler. These codes consist of pre-written classes, variables, and features to accomplish some popular duties and are stored in files known as modules. Let's look at features for the first time.

What are the features?

Functions are merely pre-written codes performing a specific job. Think of the mathematical functions in MS Excel for an analogy. Instead of typing A1+A2+A3+A4+A5, we can use the sum) (function and sort sum (A1: A5) to add numbers.

Depending on how the function is written, whether it is a component of a class (a class is an object-oriented programming notion that we are not going to address in this book) and how you import it, we can call a function merely by typing the function name or by using the dot notation. To execute their duties, some functions require us to fill in information. This information is known as parameters, and by enclosing their values in parentheses () separated by commas, we transfer them to the feature.

For example, to use the print () function to display text on the screen, we call it by typing print ("Hello World") where the print is the function name and the parameter is "Hello World."

On the other side, to use the replace () feature to manipulate text strings, we must write "Hello World," replace ("World," "Universe") where the insert is the function name and the parameters are "World" and "Universe." The string before the dot is the string that will be affected (i.e., "Hello World"). This will change "Hello World" to "Hello Universe."

Defining Your Functions

In Python, we can identify and reuse our features throughout the program. The syntax for defining a feature is as follows: deffunctionName (parameters): code specifying what the function should return[expression], def, and returned are two keywords.

Default informs the program that the indented code is a component of the feature from the next row. "Return" is the keyword we use to return a function response. In a feature, there may be more than one return statement. But once a return statement is executed by the function, the function will exit. If no value needs to be returned by your feature, you can omit the return statement. Alternatively, return or return none can be written.

Let's define our first feature now. Suppose we'd like to determine whether a specified number is a prime number. This is how the feature can be defined using the modulus (percent) operator we learned in the past section.

def check prime (number to check): for in range(2, numberToCheck): if (numberToCheck percentx= 0): return False return True

In the above feature, rows 2 and 3 use a loop to split the given numberToCheck parameter by all digits from 2 to numberToCheck-1 to determine if the remaining number is zero. The numberToCheck is not a prime number if the remaining number is zero. Line 4 returns as False and exits the feature.

If none of the division provides a remaining zero by the last iteration of the "for loop," the feature will reach Line 5 and return True. Then the feature will go out.

We type checkIfPrime(13) to use this feature and attribute it to a variable like this answer= checkIfPrime(13) Here, we pass as the parameter in 13. By typing print(answer), we can then print the response. We're going to get the result: true.

Variable Scope

The notion of variable scope is a significant notion to be understood when defining a feature. Defined variables within a function are treated differently from externally defined variables. Two primary distinctions exist.

First, any variable that is stated within a feature can only be accessed within the feature. These are referred to as local variables. Any variable declared outside a function is referred to as a global variable and can be accessed anywhere in the program.

To comprehend this, attempt the following code:

```
message1= "Global Variable"
```

```
del myFunction ():
```

```
print ("\nINSIDE THE FUNCTION") #Global variables are available
within the print function (message1)
```

```
#Local variable message2= "Local variable"
```

```
print (message2)
```

```
#Calling myFunction ()
```

```
print ("\nOUTSIDE THE FUNCTION")
```

```
#Global variables are available outside the feature
```

```
print (message1)
```

```
Print (message2)
```

You will receive the output below if you run the program.

INSIDE THE FUNCTION

Global Variable

Local variable

OUTSIDE THE FUNCTION

Global variable

NameError: name' message2' is not defined in the function, both local and global variables are accessible.

The local variable message2 is no longer available outside the feature. When we attempt to access it outside of the feature, we get a NameError.

The second concept to understand the scope of the variable is that if a local variable shares the same name as a global one, the local variable is accessed by any code within the function. The global variable is accessed by any code outside. Try to run the code below

message1= "Global Variable (shares the same name as a local variable)"

def myFunction():

message1= "Local Variable (shares the same name as a worldwide variable)"

print ("\nINSIDE THE FUNCTION")

print (message1) #Calling myFunction ()

print message1

OUTSIDE the function print ("\nOUTSIDE THE FUNCTION")

print (message1)

It accesses the global variable when we print it outside and, therefore prints "Global Variable (shares the same name as a local variable)."

Importing Modules

Python comes with a lot of built-in features. These features are stored in modules known as files, and we must first import them into our programs to use the built-in codes in Python modules. We do this by using the keyword for importing. There are three methods of doing this.

The first way is by writing import moduleName to import the entire module.

For example, we write random imports to import the random module. We write randomly.randrandrange (1, 10) to use the random () function in the random module.

Secondly, if you find it too difficult to write randomly whenever you use the feature, you can import the module by writing random imports asr (where r is any name of your decision). Now, write r.randrange (1, 10) to use the randrange () feature.

The third way to import modules is by writing from moduleName import name1[, name2[, nameN]] to import particular features from the module.

For example, we write from random import random range) (function from the random module. We separate them with a comma if we want to import more than one function. We write from random import randrange, randint, to import the random () and randint () functions. We no longer need to use the dot notation to use the feature now. Write random (1,10).

Creating our Module

We can also generate our modules in addition to importing built-in modules. This is very helpful if you have some features you would like to reuse in the future in other programming projects. It's easy to create a module. Save the file and place it in the same directory as the Python file from which you will import it.

Suppose you want to use in another Python script the check prime () feature described previously. This is how you do it. First, save the above code to your desktop as prime.py. The following code should be given to prime.py.

def checkIfPrime (numberToCheck):

for x in scope (2, numberToCheck):

if (numberToCheck percentx== 0):

return False

return True

Next, generate another Python file and use the nameCheckIfPrime.py.

Save it as well on your desktop. The following code should be used to useCheckIfPrime.py. Import prime

response= prime.checkIfPrime (13) print (answer)

Now useCheckIfPrime.py. You ought to get the True output. Simple like this.

Nevertheless, assume you want to store prime.py in separate folders and useCheckIfPrime.py. To useCheckIfPrime.py to tell the Python interpreter where to find the module, you will have to add some codes. Say you've developed a folder in your C file called 'MyPythonModules' to store prime.py., you need to add the following code (before the line import prime) to the top of your useCheckIfPrime.py file.

Import sys

if' C:\MyPythonModules' does not appear in sys.path: sys.path.append('C:\MyPythonModules ')

sys.path relates to the system route of your Python.

This is the list of directories to search for modules and files that Python is going through. The code above applies to your system path the folder ' C:\MyPythonModules.'

Now you can put prime.py in any other folder of your choice in C:\MyPythonModules and checkIfPrime.py.

Exercise

1. What are the features?

2. How can you identify a feature of your own?

3. Write down the code

4 Variables. How to import a module and generate it?

CHAPTER FIVE

FILE HANDLING

The exact file handling details differ substantially between programming languages, but virtually, all languages share some of the underlying concepts of file handling. First, we need some way to combine a disk file with a program variable. Opening a file is seen as a process. Once a file is opened, the variable we assign to it is manipulated.

Second, we need a set of activities where the file variable can be manipulated. This involves at least activities that enable us to read the data from a file and write fresh data to a file. Typically, text file read and write activities are comparable to text-based, interactive input, and output activities.

Finally, it's closed when we're done with a file. Closing a file ensures that any bookkeeping required to maintain the correspondence between the disk file and the file variable is completed. If you write data to a file variable, for instance, the modifications may not appear on the disk version until the file is closed.

This concept of opening and closing files is tightly connected to how you could work with documents like a word processor in an application program. The concepts aren't precisely the same though. The file is read from the computer and placed in RAM when you open a file in a program like Microsoft Word. The file is opened for reading activities in programming terminology. The file is closed at this stage, again in programming. You're making adjustments to information in memory as you "edit the file," not the file itself. The modifications will not appear in the disk folder until you give the command to "save" it.

There is also a multi-step method to save a file. First, the initial disk file is reopened, this time in a mode that enables information to be stored — the disk file is opened for writing. Doing so erases the file's ancient content. File writing activities are then used to copy the in-memory version's present content into the disk's fresh file. From your view, a current file appears to have been edited. From the perspective of the program, you have opened a file, read its contents into memory, closed the file, created a new file with the same name, entered the modified memory contents into the new file, and closed the new file.

It's simple to work with text files in Python. The first stage is to use the open function to connect a file to a variable.

< filevar >= open(<name >, < mode >) The name of the file on the disk is a string. Depending on whether we intend to read from the file or write to the file, the mode parameter is either the string "r" or "w."

For instance, we could use a declaration like the following to open a file on our disk called "numbers.dat" for reading.

Infile= open(' numbers.dat," r') Now, we can use the infile variable to read the numbers.dat content from the disk.

Python offers three associated file-reading activities:

<filevar>.read ()

<filevar>.readline ()

< filevar>.readlines ()

Reading returns the entire file content as a single string. The resulting string has embedded newline characters between the lines if the file contains more than one line of text.

Here is an instance program that transfers to the screen the contents of a file.

```
#Printfile.py

 #Print a screen file.

def main():

        fname= raw input(' Enter filename:')

        infile= open (fname,'r')

        data=infile.read ()

        print data

main ()
```

The program first prompts the user for a filename and then opens the variable infile file. For the variable, you could use any name. I used infile to emphasize that the file was used for input. Then the file's entire content is read as a big string and stored in the information of the variable.

Printing information creates a display of the contents.

The readline operation can be used to read a line from a file; that is, through the next newline character, it reads all the characters. Readline returns the next line from the file every time it is called. This is similar to raw input that reads characters interactively until the user reaches the < Enter > button; each raw input call receives a different line from the user. However, one thing to keep in mind is that the string returned by readline always ends with a newline character, while the newline character is discarded by raw input.

This fragment of code prints the first five lines of a file as a quick example.

Infile= open (someFile,' r')

for I in range (5):

    line = infile.readline ()

    print line[:-1]

Notice slicing at the end of the line to remove the newline character. Since printing automatically moves to the next row, i.e., a newline is produced, printing at the end with the specific newline would place an additional blank output line between the file rows.

If you want to run through all the residual rows of a file, you can use readlines as an option to readline. This procedure returns a string sequence representing the file lines. Used with a loop, processing each line of a file is a particularly useful way.

```
Infile= open (someFile,' r')

for line in infile.readlines():

        #process line here

infile.close ()
```

Prepare the file to obtain information by opening a file to write. If there is no file with the given name, it will create a fresh file. A word of warning: if there is a file with the given name, it will be removed by Python and a fresh, vacant file created. Make sure you don't clobber any documents you'll need later when writing to a file!

Here's an instance to open an output file.

```
Outfile= open ("mydata.out," "w")
```

Using the writing procedure, we can have placed information in a folder.

```
< file-var>.write (< string >)
```

This is comparable to print, unless writing is somewhat less flexible. The write procedure requires a single string parameter and returns that string to the file. If you want to start a new line in the file, the newline character must be specified explicitly.

Here is a stupid instance in which two lines are written into a file.

Outfile= open(' example.out," w')

count= 1outfile.write(' This is the first line\n')

count= count + 1

 outfile.write(' This is row number percentd' percent (count))

outfile.close ()

Notice using string formatting to write the variable count value. You need to transform it first if you want to output something that is not a string; the string formatting operator is often a useful way to do this. This code will generate a disk file called "example.out" comprising the following two lines:

This is the first line

This is line number 2

If "example. Out" existed before this fragment was executed, its ancient content was demolished.

Example Program: Batch Usernames

 Let's redo the username generation program to see how all of these parts fit together. Our prior version interactively generated usernames by having the user type in its name. If we set up accounts for a large number of users, probably not interactively, but in batch mode, the process would be done. In batch processing, files are used to input and output the program.

Our new program is designed to handle a names file. Each input file line will include a fresh user's first and last names separated by one or more spaces. The program creates an output file for each username produced containing a line.

```
#userfile.py

#Batch mode username file creation program.

Import string

def main():

 print "This program creates a username file from a"

 print "name file."

 #get the name of the file

 infileName= raw input ("What file are the names in?")

outfileName= raw input ("What file should the username go in?")

 #open the file

 infile= open (infileName,' r')
```

outfile= open(outfileName,' w')

#process each line of the input file

in infile.readlines line.

At the same moment, I have two files open for input (infile) and output (outfile).

Operating on multiple files concurrently is not uncommon for a program. I also used the reduced feature of the string library when generating the username.

This ensures the username is all inferior, even if the names of the inputs are mixed cases. Finally, the line that writes the username to the file should also be noted.

Outfile.write (uname+'\n')

To show the end of the row, you need to concatenate the newline character. Without this, all usernames in one gigantic row would run together.

Coming Attraction: Objects

Did you notice something weird about the file handling examples syntax? We use dot notation to apply an operation to a file. For instance, we type infile. Read) (to read from the infile. This is distinct from what we used before in the ordinary function application. After all, we form abs(x), not x.abs) (to take the absolute value of a variable x.

A file is an instance of an item in Python. Objects combine information with activities. The activities of an object, called methods, are invoked using the dot notation. That's why the syntax has a distinct appearance.

To be complete, I should mention that strings in Python are also objects. If you have a comparatively new Python version (2.0 or later), instead of the string library features we discussed previously, you can use string techniques. For instance, myString.split () is equivalent to string.split (myString). If this object stuff sounds confusing right now, don't worry; the next section is all about object strength (and beautiful images as well).

Exercise

1. Describe file handling.

2 In your own words. Redo any of the past programming issues using text files for input and output to make them batch-oriented.

CHAPTER SIX

OBJECTS

We've been writing programs for numbers and strings using the built-in Python data types. We saw that a certain set of values could be represented by each data type, and each had a set of related activities. In essence, we viewed the data as passive entities manipulated and combined through active operations. This is a traditional way of viewing computing. However, building complex systems helps to take a richer perspective of the data-operation relationship.

Using an object-oriented (OO) strategy, most contemporary computer programs are constructed. The orientation of the object is not easy to define. It includes several principles for developing and applying software, principles that, throughout this book, we will return to on countless occasions. This section offers a fundamental introduction through some computer graphics to object concepts.

The Object of Objects

The fundamental concept of object-oriented growth is to see a complex system as a simple object interaction. In a specific technical sense, the word objects are used here. Part of OO programming's challenge is to figure out the vocabulary. An OO object can be considered as a type of active data type that combines data and operations.

Simply put, objects understand things (they have information), and they can do things (they have activities). Through sending each other messages, objects communicate. A message is just a request for an item to do one of its activities.

Take a straightforward instance. Suppose we want a college or university information handling system to be developed. We're going to have to maintain track of significant data. To begin with, we need to maintain records of the learners attending the college. Every student could be depicted as an item in the program. Some data such as name, ID number, courses are taken, campus address, home address, GPA, etc. would be contained in a student item. It would also be possible for each student object to react to certain demands. For instance, we would have to print an email for each student to send out a mailing. A printCampusAddress procedure can handle this assignment. When sending the printCampusAddress email to a specific student object, it will print its email. A program would run through the set of student objects to print all the addresses and send each, in turn, the message of the printCampusAddress.

Other items may be referred to. Every course in the college could also be depicted by an item in our instance. Objects of the course would know things like who the instructor is, who the students are in the course, what the preconditions are, and when and where the course meets. One instance is the addition student procedure, which causes a student to be enrolled in the course. An appropriate student object would represent the student being registered. You can see how the consecutive refinement of these concepts could lead to the college's information structure being rather advanced.

You are likely not yet prepared to tackle a college information system as a starting programmer. For now, in the context of some easy graphics programming, we will study items.

GRAPHICS PROGRAMMING

Modern computer applications are not restricted to the kind of textual input and output we've used up to now. Most of the applications you know about are likely to have a so-called Graphical User Interface (GUI) that provides visual elements such as windows, icons (representative images), buttons, and menus. Interactive graphics programming can be very complex; the intricacies of graphics and graphical interfaces are dedicated to entire textbooks. GUI applications of industrial-strength are usually developed using a dedicated programming framework for graphics. Python comes with a normal Tkinter GUI module.

Tkinter is one of the easiest to use as far as GUI frameworks go, and Python is an excellent language to develop real-world GUIs. Nevertheless, taking the time to learn Tkinter would undermine the more basic job of studying the programming and design principles that this book focuses on. I wrote a graphics library (graphics.py) for use with this book to make learning simpler. This library is accessible free of charge as a Python module file1, and you are welcome to use it as you see fit. It is as easy to use the library as to place a copy of the graphics.py file in the same folder as your graphics program(s). Alternatively, in the system directory where other Python libraries are stored, you can place graphics.py so that it can be used from any file on the system.

The library of graphics makes writing simple graphics programs easy. You will, as you do, be learning principles of object-oriented programming and computer graphics that can be applied in sophisticated graphics programming environments. The graphics module information will be discussed in subsequent parts.

To whet your appetite, we will focus on a fundamental hands-on introduction. As normal, rolling up your sleeves and trying out some examples is the best way to begin learning fresh ideas.

Importing the graphics module is the first step. You can import the graphics commands into an interactive Python session if you have put graphics.py in a suitable location.

>>> Import graphics

Next, we have to build a location where the graphics will appear on the screen. That location is a graphics window or GraphWin that the graphics module provides.

>>> win= graphics. GraphWin ()

This command will create a fresh screen window. The window will be called "GraphicsWindow." GraphWin may overlap your Python interpreter window, so you may need to resize the Python window to make both of them fully visible.

The GraphWin is an object, and the variable called win is assigned to it. Through this variable, we can manipulate the window object, analogous to how file objects are manipulated by file variables. For instance, we can ruin it when we're done with a window. By issuing the close command, this is performed.

>>> win. close ()

This command will cause the window to disappear from the screen. We're going to work with quite a few graphics library commands, and it gets tedious to type the graphics. Notation whenever we use one. Python has an alternative type of import that can assist.

Import from graphics* You can load particular definitions from the library module from the declaration. You can either list the definition names to be imported or, as shown, use an asterisk to import everything that is defined in the module.

The imported commands become accessible immediately without the module name having to preface them. We can generate a GraphWin more easily after this import.

Win= Use GraphWin () using from.

Let's attempt at some drawing with our side. A graphics window is a set of small points called pixels, which is short for components of the image. We regulate what is displayed in the window by monitoring the color of each pixel. A GraphWin is 200 pixels high and 200 pixels broad by default. That implies the GraphWin has 40,000 pixels. It would be a daunting task to draw an image by assigning a color to each pixel. Instead, we're going to depend on a graphic object library. Each item sort performs its bookkeeping and understands how to draw on a GraphWin.

The graphics module's easiest object is a point. In geometry, a point is a room/place without dimensions. A point is situated by a coordinate system reference. Our Point graphics object is comparable; it can depict a GraphWin place. By providing x and y coordinates (x, y), we describe a point.

The x value represents the point's horizontal position, and the y value represents the vertical position.

Graphics programmers traditionally find the Point (0,0) in the window's upper-left corner. This increases x values from left to right and y values from top to bottom. The lower-right corner has the coordinates in the default 200x 200 GraphWin (199, 199). Drawing a Point sets the appropriate pixel color in the GraphWin. The default diagram color is black.

Here is a sample interaction with Python that illustrates Points use.

```
>>> p= Point (50,60)
>>> p.getX ()
50
>>> p.getY ()
60
```

>>> win= GraphWin () >>> p.draw (win)

>>> p2= Point (140,100)

>>>p2.draw (win)

The first row produces a Point situated at (50, 60)

After the Point is formed, its coordinate values can be obtained through the getX and getY activities. Using the drawing procedure, a point is drawn into a window.

In this instance, it creates and draws two distinct point items (p and p2) into the GraphWin called win. The graphics library includes instructions for drawing lines, circles, rectangles, ovals, polygons, and text in relation to Points. Similarly, each of these objects is developed and drawn. Here's a sample interaction to draw a GraphWin into different forms.

>>> ####Open a graphics window

>>> win= GraphWin ('Shapes')

>>> #####Draw a red circle centered at point (100,100) with a radius of 30

>>> middle= point (100,100)

>>> circ= circle (centre, 30)

>>> circ.setFill(' red')

```
>>>circ.draw (win)

>>> ####Put a text tag in the center of the circle

>>> label= text (centre,' red circle')

>>>label.draw (win)

>>> #####Draw a square using an object

>>> rectangle= Rectangle (Point (30,30), Point (70,70))

>>>rect.draw (win)

>>> #####Draw a line section using a line object

>>> line= line (Point (20,30), Point (180, 165)))

>>> line.draw (win)

>>> ### Draw an oval using an oval object

>>> oval= oval (Point (20,150), Point (180,199)))

>>>oval.draw (win)
```

USING GRAPHICAL OBJECTS

We need to take an object-oriented point of perspective to comprehend the graphics module. Recall objects merge activities with information. Computing is done by requesting an object to perform one of its activities. You need to understand how to produce them and how to request activities to make use of objects.

We manipulated several distinct types of objects in the interactive examples above: GraphWin, Point, Circle, Oval, Line, Text, and Rectangle. These are class examples. Each object is a class instance, and the class describes the properties that the instance will have. When we say that Fido is a dog, we effectively say that Fido is a particular person in the bigger class of all dogs, borrowing a biological metaphor. Fido is an instance of the dog class in OO terminology.

We expect certain things because Fido is an instance of this class. Fido's got four legs, a tail, a cold, moist nose and he's barking. If Rex is a dog, we expect to have comparable characteristics, although Fido and Rex may vary in particular information such as size or color. Our computational objects have the same ideas. We can set up two distinct Point cases, say p and p2. Each of these points has a value of x and y, both of which support the same set of activities as get X and draw. These properties hold due to Points being the objects. However, in particular, details such as the values of their coordinates, different instances may vary.

We use a unique procedure called a constructor to generate a fresh class example. A call to a builder is an expression creating a brand new item. The overall shape is the following.

< class-name>(<param1 >, < param2 >,...)

Here < class-name > is the name of the class we want to create, e.g. Circle or Point, a new instance. The parentheses expressions are any parameters necessary to initialize the object. The parameter amount and type relies on the class. A point requires two numerical values, while without any parameters a GraphWin can be constructed. Typically, on the correct side of an assignment statement, a constructor is used and the resulting object is immediately allocated to a variable on the left side which is then used to manipulate the object.

Let's look at what happens when we generate a graphical point to take a concrete instance. Here is a declaration of the constructor from the above interactive instance.

P= Point (50,60) The Point class constructor requires two parameters of x and y for the new point.

These values are stored within the item as instance variables. In this situation, Python produces a Point example with a 50x value and a 60 y value. Variable p is then allocated the resulting point. Note that only the most outstanding details are shown in this diagram as well as comparable ones later on. Points also comprise other data such as color and the window, if any, in which they are displayed. When the Point is formed, most of this data is set to default values.

We send a message to the object to perform an operation on an object. The set of texts to which an object reacts is called the object's methods. Methods can be thought of as features that reside within the item. Using dot notation, a technique is invoked.

< object>.<method-name>(<param1 >, < param2 >,...)

The technique used determines the amount and type of parameters. Certain techniques do not involve any parameters. In the interactive examples above, you can find numerous examples of the method invocation.

Take these two phrases as examples of parameterless techniques.

P.getX ()

p.getY ()

Return the x and y values of a Point respectively by the get X and get Y techniques. Such methods are sometimes referred to as **accessors**, as they enable us to access data from the object's instance variables.

Other techniques alter the values of the instance variables of an item, thus altering the object's status.

All graphic objects have a technique of moving. Here is a specification: move (dx, dy): move the dx units of the item in the x direction and dy units in the y direction.

We could use this declaration to transfer Point p to the correct 10 units.

P.move (10,0)

By adding 10 units, this changes the x instance variable of p. If the Point in a GraphWin is presently drawn, move will also take care to erase the ancient picture and draw it in its fresh place. Methods that change an object's state are sometimes referred to as **mutators**.

The movement technique must have two easy numerical parameters showing the distance to move the object along each dimension. Some techniques involve parameters that are complicated items themselves. For instance, two items are involved in drawing a Circle into a GraphWin. Let's look at a series of instructions for doing this.

Circle= Circle (Point (100,100), 30)

Win= GraphWin ()

circ.draw (win)

Circle with the core at Point (100,100) and radius of 30. Notice, we used the Point Builder to generate a place for the Circle Builder's first parameter. A GraphWin is created by the second row. See what's going on in the third row? This is a request to draw itself into the GraphWin object win for the Circle object circ. This statement's noticeable impact is a circle centered at (100, 100) in the GraphWin with a radius of 30. There's a lot more going on behind the scenes.

Remember, inside the circ item, the draw technique lives. Using data from the example factors about the middle and radius of the circle, the drawing technique issues a suitable series of low-level drawing instructions (a sequence of method invocations) to the GraphWin. Fortunately, we usually don't have to worry about such information; the graphic items take care of them all. We are creating items, calling the suitable techniques and letting them do the job. That's the strength of programming focused on objects. You need to maintain in mind one subtle "gotcha" when using items. It is feasible to refer to precisely the same object for two distinct factors; changes made to the object will also be notified to the other variable. Suppose we try to write a code sequence that draws a smiley face. We want to produce two eyes separated by 20 units.

Choosing Coordinates

In designing the futval graph program, the lion's share of the work was in determining the exact coordinates where things would be placed on the screen. Most graphics programming issues involve some kind of coordinate transformation to alter values from a real-world issue to window coordinates that are mapped to the computer screen. In our example,x values representing the year (0–10) and y values representing monetary amounts ($0–$10,000) were called for by the problem domain. To be depicted in a 320x 240 window, we had to convert these values. Working through an example or two is nice to see how this transformation is going on, but it makes programming tedious.

Coordinate transformation is a component of computer graphics that is integral and well-studied. To see that the conversion method always follows the same overall pattern does not take too much mathematical expertise. It is possible to do anything that follows a pattern automatically. To save you the trouble of having to explicitly convert between coordinate systems back and forth, the graphics module provides you with a simple mechanism to do that. Using the setCoords technique, you can indicate a window coordinate scheme when creating a GraphWin. The technique needs four parameters to specify the lower-left and upper-right corner coordinates, respectively. This coordinate system can then be used to place graphical objects in the window.

Suppose we want to divide the window into nine equal squares, Tic-Tac-Toe fashion, to take a simple example. Using the default 200x 200 window, this could be achieved without too much difficulty, but it would involve some arithmetic. When we first change the window coordinates to run from 0 to 3 in both dimensions, the problem becomes trivial.

#Create the default 200x200 window

win = GraphWin('Tic-Tac-Toe')

#set the coordinates from (0,0) at the bottom left

#to (3,3) at the top end.

Win.setCoords(0.0, 0.0, 3.0, 3.0)

#Draw vertical lines

Line (point (1,0), point (1,3)).draw (win)

107

Line (point (2,0), point (2,3)).draw (win)

#Draw horizontal lines

Line (point (0,1), point (3,1)).draw (win)

Line (point (0,2), point (3,2)).draw (win))

Another advantage of this strategy is that the size of the window can be altered by merely altering the sizes used when the window was formed (e.g. The objects will scale properly to the fresh window size because the same coordinates span the window (owing to setCoords). Using "raw" window coordinates would involve modifications in line definitions.

To simplify our future value graphing program, we can apply this concept. Basically, we want our graphics window to go from 0 to 10 in the x dimension (representing years) and from 0 to 10,000 in the y dimension (representing usd). We could just generate such a window.

win= GraphWin('Investment Growth Chart', 320, 240)

win.setCoords(0.0, 0.0, 10.0, 10000.0)

Then it would be easy to create a bar for any year and main values. At the given year, each bar starts with a baseline of 0 and grows to the next year and a height equal to the main one.

Bar= Rectangle (Point(year,0),Point(year+1, main))

This system has a tiny issue. Can you see what I forgot? The bars will fill the whole window; we have left no space around the corners for labels or margins. This is readily solved by slightly extending the window coordinates. We can find the left side labels at-1 since our bars begin at 0. By extending the coordinates slightly beyond what our graph requires, we can add some white space around the graph. A small experimentation leads to this definition of the window: win= GraphWin ("Investment Growth Chart," 320, 240) win.setCoords(-1.75,-200, 11.5, 10400)

Interactive Graphics

Graphical interfaces can be used for both input and output. Users typically communicate with their apps in a GUI setting by clicking on buttons, selecting menu items, and typing data into text boxes on the screen. These apps are using a programming method called event-driven. The program draws on the screen a set of interface components (often referred to as widgets) and then expects the user to do something.

This produces an incident when the user moves the mouse, clicks on a button, or forms a key on the keyboard. An event is an object that encapsulates information on what has just occurred. The object of the case will then be sent to a suitable portion of the program to be processed. A click on a button, for instance, could result in a button case. This event would be carried to the handling code button, which would then execute that button's suitable action.

Event-driven programming can be difficult for novice programmers as it is difficult at any given time to find out who is in charge. The graphics module hides the fundamental processes for event handling and offers two easy methods to get user input into a GraphWin.

Getting Mouse Clicks

We can use the GraphWin class getMouse method to obtain graphical information from the user. The program pauses and waits for the user to click the mouse somewhere in the graphics window when get Mouse is invoked on a GraphWin. The location where the user clicks are returned as a point to the program.

Here's a bit of software reporting the 10 consecutive mouse click co-ordinates.

For i in range (10):

 p= win.getMouse ()

print "You clicked (percent d, percent d)" percent (p.getX), (p.getY ())

The value returned by getMouse () is a ready-made point. Using accessors like getX and get Y or other methods like draw and move, we can use it like any other point.

Displaying Images

The graphics module also offers minimal assistance to display certain picture formats in a GraphWin.

Most platforms support images from JPEG, PPM, and GIF. An Image object is displayed. Images support moving(dx, dy), draw(graphwin), undraw), (and clone) (generic methods. Specific techniques for the image are shown below.

Image (centerPoint, filename) Builds an image centered at the given center point from the contents of the given file.

GetAnchor) (Returns the point-centered clone of the picture.

Strings are used to generate colors. There should be most common colors such as 'red," purple," green," cyan,' etc. Many colors come in different shades, like' red1," red2," red3," red4,' which are becoming darker red tones.

The graphics module also offers a feature for numerically blending your own colors. The rgb (red, green, blue) function returns a string representing a color that is a mix of specified red, green and blue intensities. These should be in the 0−255 range. Thus rgb (255,0, 0) is a bright red color, whereas rgb (130,0, 130) is a medium magenta color.

1. Choose an example of an interesting object in the real world and describe it as a programming object by listing its data (attributes, what it "knows") and methods (behaviors, what it can do).

2. Describe what happens when the following program is running interactive graphics.

Win= GraphWin) (shape= Circle(Point(50,50), 20) shape.setOutline('red') shape.setFill('red') shape.draw(win) for I in range(10): p=win.getMouse) (c= shape.getCenter) (dx= p.getX)(= c.getX) (dy= p.getY)(− c.getY) (shape.move(dx,dy) win.close)

CHAPTER SEVEN

Defining Classes

We have created methods to structure a program's computations. We will look at techniques for structuring the data used by our programs in the next few chapters. You already understand that objects are a significant instrument for complicated data management. Our programs have used items generated from predefined classes like Circle to date. You will learn how to write your courses in this section in order to generate new items.

Quick Review of Objects Recall back in Chapter 5 that I defined an object as an active type of data that knows things and can do things.

More specifically, an item is made up of 1. A collection of data linked to this.

2. A set of manipulating these information operations.

In instance variables, the information is stored inside the object. The activities, called methods, are functions within the item that is "living." Collectively, an object's attributes are called the instance variables and methods.

To take a familiar example now, a Circle object will have instance variables such as the center that recalls the center point of the circle, and the radius that stores the length of the radius of the circle. The circle's techniques will need this information to carry out activities. The drawing technique examines the middle and radius to determine which pixels are to be colored in a window. The movement technique will alter the center value to represent the circle's current position.

Remember that each item is said to be a class example. The object's class determines what the object will have characteristics. A class is a description of what will be known and done by its cases. By invoking a constructor, new objects are created from a class. You can see the class itself as a kind of factory to stamp out fresh cases.

Consider creating a fresh circle object: myCircle= Circle(Point(0,0), 20) Circle, the class name, is used to invoke the builder. This declaration generates a fresh example of the Circle and stores a reference in the myCircle variable. The constructor parameters are used to initialize some of the instance factors within myCircle (i.e. center and radius). Once the example is formed, it will be manipulated by calling its methods: myCircle.draw(win) myCircle.move(dx, dy) ...

Before we start a thorough debate on how to write your own courses, let's take a brief detour to see how helpful the Cannonball program can be to use fresh courses.

Program Specification - Suppose we want to write a program that simulates a cannonball's flight (or any other projectile such as putting a bullet, baseball or shot). We are especially interested in figuring out how far the cannonball will move when it is shot at different starting angles and original speeds. The program input will be the start angle in degrees, the original speed in meters per second and the original height in meters. The yield will be the distance the projectile travels (in meters) before hitting the floor.

If we ignore the effects of wind resistance and assume that the cannonball remains close to the surface of the earth, i.e., we don't try to put it in orbit, this is a relatively simple problem of classical Physics. The gravity acceleration near the surface of the earth is about 9.8 meters per second. This implies that if an object is thrown up at a velocity of 20 meters per second, its upward velocity will slow down to 20 −9.8= 10.2 meters per second after one second has passed. The velocity will be only 0.4 meters per second after another second, and soon after that, it will begin to come back down.

It's not difficult for those who understand a bit of Calculus to derive a formula that provides our cannonball's place at any specified time in their flight. However, instead of taking the strategy to calculus, our program will use simulation to monitor the time of cannonball. We can solve this problem algorithmically by using just a little simple trigonometry to get started, together with the obvious relationship that the distance an object travels in a given amount of time is equal to its rate times the amount of time (d= rt).

Let's start with designing an algorithm for this issue. It is evident from the issue declaration that we need to consider the cannonball flight in two aspects: height, so we know when it reaches the floor, and distance, to maintain track of how far it goes. We can believe the cannonball's place as a Point (x, y) in a 2D graph where the y value provides the height and thex value provides the starting point distance.

To account for its flight, our simulation will have to update the cannonball's position. Suppose the ball begins at the place (0,0), and we want, say, every quarter of a second, to verify its place. It will have shifted up a certain distance (positive y) and a certain pace forward (positive x) in that interval. The precise distance in each dimension is determined in that direction by its velocity.

Separating the velocities of x and y parts makes the issue simpler. The x velocity stays continuous for the entire flight as we ignore the wind resistance. The y velocity, however, shifts over time owing to the gravity impact. In reality, as the cannonball begins to fall back down, the y velocity will begin to be positive and then become negative.

Because of this assessment, what our simulation will have to do is fairly evident. Here's a rough overview: input the parameters of the simulation: angle, speed, height, and interval.

Calculate the initial position of the cannonball: xpos, ypos Calculate the initial velocities of the cannonball: xvel, yvel While the cannonball is still flying: update the values of xpos, ypos, and yvel for interval seconds further in the flight Output the distance traveled as xpos Let's turn this into a program using step-by-step refinement.

The algorithm's first line is simple. We only need a suitable series of statements of input.

Enter the start angle (in degrees):') vel= input(' Enter the original speed (in meters / sec):') ho= input(' Enter the original height (in meters):') time= input(' Enter the time interval between position calculations:')

Defining New Classes

Let's take an even simpler example to examine the basic ideas before designing a Projectile class.

Example: Multi-Sided Dice

You know an ordinary die is a cube and each face displays a number from one to six. Some matches use non-standard dice with fewer (for example, four) or more (for example, thirteen) sides. Let's design a general MSDie class to model multi-sided dice.1 In any amount of simulation programs or game programs, we could use such an item.

Every object of MSDie knows two things.

1. How many sides there are.

2. Its actual value.

We indicate how many sides it will have when creating a fresh MSDie, n. Then we can operate on the die using three methods provided: roll, setting the die to a random value between 1 and n, inclusive; setValue, setting the die to a specific value (i.e. cheat); and getValue, seeing the current value.

Here's an interactive example showing what our class will do:

```
>>> die1= MSDie(6)

>>> die1.getValue ()

1

>>> die1.roll ()

>>> die1.getValue ()

4

>>> die2= MSDie(13)

>>> die2.getValue ()

1

>>> die2.getValue ()

>>> die2.getValue ()

12

>>> die2.getValue(8)

>>> die2.getValue ()

8
```

See how useful it might be? I can define any number of dice with arbitrary siding numbers. Each die can be spun separately and will always generate a random value determined by the amount of sides within the correct range. By invoking the MSDie constructor and giving the amount of sides as a parameter, we generate a die using our object-oriented terminology. Our die object uses an instance variable to keep track of this number internally. To store the die's current value, another instance variable will be used. Initially, the die value is set to 1, as this is a legal value for any die. The value can be altered and returned from the getValue technique by the roll and setRoll techniques.

It is quite simple to write a definition for the MSDie class. A class is a collection of methods and only functions are methods. Here is MSDie's class description:

#msdie.py

#A n-sided die's class definition.

From the random import random class MSDie:

```
 def init (self, sides):

 self.sides = sides

self.value = 1

def roll(self):

self.value = randrange (1,self.sides+1)

 def getValue(self):

return self.value
```

```
def setValue (self, value):

self.value = value
```

As you can see, a class definition has a straightforward shape: class <class-name>: <method-definitions> Each method definition looks like a standard function definitio. Placing the feature within a class makes it a class method rather than a stand-alone function.

Let's take a look at this class's three-technique. You will realize that each technique has a self-named first parameter. A method's first parameter is special— it always includes a reference to the item the method acts on. As normal, for this parameter, you can use any name you want but the traditional name is self, so that's what I'm always going to use.

An instance could be useful in self-realization. Suppose we have a major feature running die1.setValue(8). An invocation technique is a call to the feature. As in ordinary function calls, a four-step sequence is executed by Python:

1. The calling program (primary) is suspended at the implementation stage of the technique. Python locates the suitable method definition within the object class to which the technique is applied. In this case, control is transferred to the MSDie class setValue method because die1 is an MSDie instance.

2. The method's formal parameters are allocated to the values provided by the call's real parameters. The first formal parameter refers to the

item in the event of a method call. In our instance, before executing the method body, it is as if the following tasks are completed: self= die1 value= 8

3. The method's body is performed.

4. In this case, the statement immediately after die1.setValue(8) returns to the point just after the method was called.

Notice how one parameter (the value) is used to call the technique but the process definition has two parameters because of itself. We'd say that setValue needs one parameter in general. A bookkeeping detail is the self-parameter in the definition. This is implicitly done by some languages; Python requires us to add the extra parameter. I will always refer to the first formal parameter of a method as the self-parameter and any other parameters as normal parameters to avoid confusion. So, I'd say setValue uses one parameter that is normal.

Some techniques have a unique significance for Python in a class. The names of these techniques start and end with two underscores. The init unique technique is the constructor of the item. To initialize a fresh MSDie, Python calls this technique. Init's function is to provide original values for an object's instance variables.

From outside the class, the name of the class refers to the constructor.

Die1= MSDie(6)

Python generates a fresh MSDie and executes init on that item when executing this declaration. The net outcome is the setting of die1.sides to 6 and die1.value to 1.

The strength of instance variables is that we can use them to remember a specific object's state, and this data is then transferred as part of the object around the program. In other techniques or even in consecutive calls to the same technique, the values of instance variables can be referenced again. This is distinct from periodic local function variables, the values of which vanish when the function ends.

Here is a straightforward illustration:

>>> die1= Die(13)

>>>print die1.getValue ()

1

>>> die1.setValue(8)

>>> print die1.getValue ()

8

Instance variable die1.value is set to 1 by calling the constructor. This value is printed out in the next row.

As part of the object, the value set by the constructor persists, even though the constructor is finished with it, similarly, by setting the value to 8, executing die1.setValue(8) changes the item. When the next time you ask the item for its value, it reacts with 8.

That's just about everything Python needs to understand about identifying fresh courses. Now it's time to make use of this fresh understanding.

Encapsulating Useful Abstractions

Hopefully, you can see how a useful way to modularize a program can be to define fresh courses. Once we recognize some items that may help solve a specific issue, we can write an algorithm as if we had those objects accessible and move the information of the application into an appropriate class definition. This provides us the same sort of separation of issues we used in top-down design tasks. The primary program has only to be concerned about what objects can do, not how they are applied.

Computer scientists call this encapsulation, separation of interests. The details of an object's implementation are encapsulated in the class definition, which isolates the rest of the program from dealing with it. This is another abstraction implementation (ignoring irrelevant information), which is the core of the excellent design.

I should mention that encapsulation is just a Python programming convention. The language does not enforce it per se. We included two brief techniques in our Projectile class, get X, and get Y, which merely returned the values of xpos and ypos instance variables, respectively. These techniques are not absolutely essential, strictly speaking. In Python, with periodic dot notation, you can access any object's instance variables. For example, by creating an object and then directly inspecting the values of the instance variables, we could interactively test the constructor for the Projectile class.

>>> c= Projectile(60, 50, 20)

```
>>> c.xpos

0.0

>>> c.ypos

20

>>> c.xvel

25.0

>>> c.yvel

 43.301270
```

One of the primary reasons objects are used is to isolate programs that use these items from the inner information of how they are performed. References to example variables should stay with the remainder of application information within the class definition. Our interaction with an item should be carried out from outside the class using the interface supplied by its techniques. You should endeavor to provide a full set of techniques to make your class helpful as you design your courses. Thus, other programs need not understand about or manipulate inner information such as variables of instances.

Putting Classes in Modules

A well-defined class or set of classes often provide helpful abstractions that can be leveraged in many separate programs. We may want to turn our projectile class into its module file for other programs to use. In doing so, it would be a good idea to add paperwork that explains how to use the class to prevent programmers who want to use the module from studying the code to find out or remember what the class and its techniques are doing.

One way to document programs is already familiar to you: comments. Providing remarks explaining the contents of a module and its uses is always a good idea. In reality, such remarks are so essential that Python includes a unique kind of convention called a **docstring** for commenting. To document that element, you can insert a simple string literally as the first line of a module, class or function.

The advantage of docstrings is that while Python ignores ordinary comments, docstrings are carried along in a special attribute called docduring execution. It is possible to examine these strings dynamically. Most Python library modules have extensive docstrings to help you use the module or its contents. For example, if you are unable to remember how to use the random range function, you can print your docstring as follows: >>> import random >>> print random.randrange. doc   Select a random item from range(start, stop[, step]).

Here is a variant of our Projectile class as a module file with docstrings included: #projectile.py"

"projectile.py

Provides a straightforward class for projectile flight modeling." "from math import pi, sin, cos

Widget Objects

A popular use of objects is the design of graphical user interfaces (GUIs). We talked about visual interface objects consisting of GUIs called widgets. An instance of a widget is the Entry object defined in our graphics library. We can generate our custom widgets now that we understand how to identify fresh courses.

Example Program: Dice Roller

Let's attempt to build a few helpful widgets with our hands. Consider a program that rolls a couple of normal (six-sided) dice as an instance implementation. The program will graphically show the dice and provide two buttons, one to roll the dice and one to quit the program. Figure 10.3 displays a user interface snapshot.

You can see that there are two types of widgets in this program: buttons and dice. We can begin with the development of appropriate courses. The two buttons will be button class cases, and DieView will be the class that gives a graphical perspective of a die's value.

Building Buttons

Buttons are, of course, virtually every GUI's standard elements these days. Modern buttons are very advanced; they generally look and feel three-dimensional. Our easy graphics package has no equipment to generate buttons that appear to depress when clicked. The best we can do is find out where the mouse paused after completing the button. Nevertheless, we can create a class of buttons helpful, if less beautiful.

Our buttons in a graphics window will be rectangular areas where user clicks can affect the running application's conduct. We're going to need to build buttons and determine when they clicked. Furthermore, being able to activate and deactivate individual buttons is also great. Thus, our apps can, at any specified time, indicate which alternatives are accessible to the user. Inactive buttons are typically grayed out to demonstrate that they are not accessible.

To summarize this description, the following methods will be supported by our buttons: Creating a key in a window. The window in which the button will be displayed, the location/size of the button, and the label on the button will need to be specified.

Activate the Set button status to enable.

Deactivate Set the inactive status of the button.

Clicked Specify if you clicked the button. This technique will determine if the point is active if the button is active.

> Clicked in the region of the button. The point must be sent to the technique as a parameter.

GetLabel Returns the button's label string. This is given to recognize a specific button.

EXERCISES

1. Use the button class mentioned in this section to create a GUI from past chapters for one (or more) of your projects.

2. Write a class of modified buttons creating circular buttons.

CHAPTER EIGHT

MAKING CHOICES AND DECISIONS

Congratulations to you as you've shaped into another interesting section. I hope that so far, you liked the course. In this section, we will examine how to create your program to be more intelligent and able to create choices and decisions. In particular, we're going to look at the "if statement," the loop, and the loop. These are called tools for controlling flow; they regulate the program flow. We will also look at the trial, except for a declaration that determines what the program is supposed to do when an error happens.

However, we must first look at statements of conditions before we go into these control flow instruments.

Condition Statement

All control flow instruments require assessing a declaration of condition. Depending on whether the condition is satisfied, the program will continue differently.

The most popular declaration of conditions is the declaration of comparison. We use the== sign (double =) if we want to compare whether two variables are the same. For example, if you write x== y, you ask the program to check whether the value ofx is equal to the value of y. If they are equivalent, the situation will be encountered, and

True will be assessed by the declaration. Else, False will assess the declaration.

Other indications of comparison include! (not equal to), < (less than), > (higher than), <= (less than or equal to) and >= (higher than or equal to). The list below shows how to use these signs and provides examples of statements that True will evaluate.

Not the same as: 5! 2 Larger than: 5>2 Larger than: 2<5 Larger than or equal to: 5>=2 5>=5 Larger than or equal to: 2 <= 5 <= 2 Larger than or equal to: 2 <= 5 2 <= 2 Logical operators are also available and are not helpful if various circumstances are to be combined. The operator returns True if all requirements are fulfilled. Otherwise, False's going to return. For example, statements 5==5 and 2>1 are going to return True as both conditions are True.

If at least one condition is met, the or operator returns True. Otherwise, False's going to return. The declaration 5 > 2 or 7 > 10 or 3== 2 returns True as the first condition 5>2 is True. If the situation after the not keyword is incorrect, the non-operator returns True. Otherwise, False's going to return. The declaration not 2>5 will return True as 2 will not exceed 5.

If Statement

The if statement is one of the control flow statements most frequently used. It enables the program to assess whether a certain condition is met and to take suitable action based on the assessment consequence. The if statement structure is as follows: if condition 1 is fulfilled: do A elif condition 2: do B elif condition 3 is fulfilled: do C elif condition 4 is fulfilled: do D else: do Elif stands for "otherwise if" and you can have as many elif statements as you want.

If you have previously coded in other languages such as C or Java, you may be amazed to notice that after the if, elif and other keyword, no parentheses) (are required in Python. Moreover, Python does not use curly{} brackets to describe the if statement begin and end. Python is using indentation rather. Any indented thing is treated as a code block that will be executed if the condition is true.

To fully comprehend how the declaration operates, use the following code to shoot IDLE and key.

UserInput= input(' Enter 1 or 2:') if userInput== "1": print ("Hello World") print ("How are you?") elif userInput== "2": print ("Python Rocks!") print ("I love Python") otherwise: print ("You did not enter a valid amount").

The results are collected as a string in the userInput variable. Next the userInput== "1" declaration: compares the userInput variable with the "1" string. If the value stored in userInput is "1," all statements indented will be executed by the program until the indentation finishes. It will print "Hello World" in this instance, followed by "How are you?".

If the value stored in userInput is "2," the program will also print "Python Rocks" and "I love Python." The program will print "You didn't enter a valid amount" for all other values.

Run the program three times, enter 1, 2, and 3 for each run respectively.

The following output will be given to you: Enter 1 or 2: 1 Hello World. How are you?

Enter 1 or 2: 2 rocks of Python!

I love Python Enter 1 or 2:3 You haven't entered a valid number

Inline If

An inline if declaration is an easier type of a declaration and is more convenient if you only need to do a straightforward job. The syntax is: do Task A if situation is true else do Task B For example, number1= 12 ifmyInt==10 else 13 If myInt is equal to 10, this declaration assigns 12 to number1 (Task A). Apart from that, it assigns 13 to num1 (Task B).

Another instance is print ("This is Task A" if myInt== 10 "Task B") This statement prints "Task A" if myInt is equal to 10. Otherwise, "This is Task B" (Task B) is printed.

Let's look at the for loop for Loop Next. The for loop executes a block of code continuously until it no longer validates the situation in the declaration for.

Looping through an iterable

In Python, an iterable refers to anything, such as a string, list or tuple, that can be looped over. The syntax for looping through an iterable is as follows:

for an in iterable:

print (a)

Example: pets=[' cats," dogs," rabbits,'" hamsters'] for myPets in pets: print (myPets)

In the above program, we declare the list pets first and give it to the members ' cats," dogs," rabbits' and' hamsters.' Next the statement for myPets in animals: runs through the list of animals and assigns the variable myPets to each member in the list. It assigns' cats' to the variable myPets the first time the program passes through the for loop. Printing the statement (myPets) then prints the' cats ' value. The second time the programs loops through the for statement, it assigns the value' dogs' to myPets and prints the value' dogs'. The program continues looping through the list until the end of the list is reached.

If you run the program, you will receive hamsters from cats dogs rabbits We can also show the members index in the list. To do that, we use the function enumerate).

For index, myPets in enumerate(pets): print (index, myPets) This gives us the output of 0 cats 1 dogs 2 rabbits 3 hamsters The following instance demonstrates how to loop through a string.

Message=' Hello'

for i in message:

print (i)

The output is

Hello

Looping through a series of numbers

The built-in range () feature is useful to loop through a series of numbers. The function range () generates a number list and has the range of syntaxes (start, end, step).

If no start is given, the generated numbers will start at zero.

Note: A helpful tip to remember here is that we always begin from zero in Python (and most programming languages), unless indicated otherwise.

For example, a list index and a tuple start at zero. The parameter positions begin from zero when using the format) (technique for strings.

If the start is not specified, the numbers generated start from zero when using the range () function.

If the step is not specified, it will generate a list of successive figures (i.e. step= 1). It is necessary to provide the final value. One strange thing about the range) (function, however, is that the end value provided is never a component of the produced list.

For example, range (5) generates a list[0, 1, 2, 3, 4] range (3, 10) generates[3, 4, 5, 6, 7, 8, 9] range (4, 10, 2) generates[4, 6, 8] To see how the range () function works in a statement, try running the following code: for I in range (5): print I 01234 While Loop The next control flow statement we're going to look at is the while loop. A while loop repeatedly executes instructions inside the loop, as the name suggests, while a certain condition remains valid. A while statement's structure is as follows: while the condition is true: do A Most of the moment when using a while loop, we first need to declare a variable to work as a loop counter. Let's just call this counter variable. In the while declaration, the situation will assess the counter value to determine whether it is lower (or larger) than a certain value. If it is, execute the loop. Let's look at a program of samples.

Counter= 5 while counter > 0: print ("Counter=" counter) counter= counter-1 If the program is running, the following output counter= 5 counter= 4 counter= 3 counter= 2 counter= 1

At first glance, a while statement appears to be the simplest syntax and should be the easiest to use. However, owing to the risk of infinite loops, one has to be cautious when using while loops. Notice that we have the line counter= counter-1 in the above program? This is a key line. It lowers counter value by 1 and gives this fresh value back to counter by overwriting the initial value.

We need to reduce counter value by 1 so that False ultimately evaluates the loop situation while countering> 0. If we forget to do that, the loop will continue to run endlessly leading to an infinite loop. Just remove the row counter= counter-1 and attempt running the program again if you want to experience this first hand. The program will continue to print counter= 5 until you destroy the program in some way. Especially if you have a large program and you have no idea which code segment causes the infinite loop, it is not a pleasant experience.

Break When working with loops, sometimes when a certain situation is encountered, you may want to leave the whole loop. We use the break keyword to do that.

Run the program below to see how it operates.

J= o for I in range (5): j= j+ 2(' I=', I', j=', j) if j== 6: break The following yield should be obtained.

I= o, j= 2 I= 1, j= 4 I= 2, j= 6

The program should loop from I= o to I= 4 without the break keyword because the function range (5) was used. The program finishes early at I= 2 with the break keyword, though. This is because if I= 2, j will reach the value of 6 and the keyword break will cause the loop to end.

Notice that we used an if statement within a loop in the example above. In programming, it is very common for us to' mix-and-match' different control tools, such as using a while loop inside an if statement or using a loop inside a while loop. This is regarded as an indication of nested control.

Continue The continuing keyword is another helpful keyword for loops. If we proceed using the remainder of the loop will be skipped for that iteration after the keyword. An example is going to make it clearer.

J= 0 for I in scope (5): j= j+ 2 printing(' \ni=', I', j=', j) if j== 6: proceed printing(' I'm skipping over if j=6') You get the following output: I= 0, j= 2 I'm skipping over if j=6 I= 1, j= 4 I'm skipping over if j=6 I= 2, j= 6 I= 3, j= 8 I'm skipping over if j=6 I= 4, j= 10 I'm skipping over if j=6 If j= 6, the row after the continuous keyword is n= 6. Other than that, it all operates as usual.

WORKING WITH DATES AND TIMES

The datetime package of Python is a convenient set of dates and times tools. You can manage most of your datetime processing requirements with just the five tricks that I'm about to demonstrate you.

Wrangling dates and times in the datetime package of python Python is a convenient set of dates and times tools. You can handle most of your datetime processing needs with just the five tricks that I'm about to show you.

It is useful to look at how datetime is set up before jumping in. A datetime object is the basic construction block. Not amazingly, this is a mixture between a date object and a time object. A date object is just a set of values for the year, the month, the day, and a set of functions that know how to handle it. A time object is similarly organized. It has hour, minute, second, microsecond values and time zone values. By selecting these values properly, any time can be depicted.

1. Combine ()

import datetime

#(hours, minutes)

start time= datetime.time(7, 0)

#(year, month, day)

start date= datetime.date(2015, 5, 1)

#Create a datetime object

start datetime= datetime.datetime.combine(start date, start time)

The first trick is to combine date and time objects to create them. We start by creating a time, going through the 7 hour and the 0 minute. This represents 7 a.m. Because we did not supply the second or microsecond, it is assumed that this is zero. Then, by passing year, month, and day, we create a date. It is easy to create a datetime. We use the combine) (function to pass the date object and the time object from which we want our datetime to be constructed.

Calls to datetime may be confusing due to the naming convention. Datetime is the package name, the package module and the object. So we call it with the apparently redundant datetime.datetime prefix when we combine our date with time. The first datetime refers to the package, the second datetime refers to the module and combine) (is a module function.

2. Timedelta

#Timedelta objects are differences between date times.

Timedelta total= end datetime-start datetime

#timedeltas have days, seconds and microseconds

#Dates and times increment, #date and time zone quirks.

End datetime= start datetime + timedelta total Type timedelta is the second trick to use datetimes. This is the distinction between two datetimes. There are three values in a timedelta: days, seconds and microseconds. In this manner, the distinction between any two date times can be depicted uniquely.

Timedeltas are extremely helpful as they enable us to do easy datetime arithmetic addition and subtraction. They remove the need to think about things like the number of days in a month, the number of seconds in a day, and the number of leap years.

3. Timestamps

#Number of seconds from 12:00 am, 1 January 1970, UTC #is a computer-friendly way of managing time.

Unix epoch= start datetime= fromtimestamp(1457453760) The third trick to get the most out of date times is to use timestamps. It is uncomfortable for computers to work in days, hours, minutes, and seconds. Checking rules and cases in the corner. To make it easier to work with dates and times, the notion of an UNIX epoch has been created. This is the amount of seconds gone in Coordinated Universal Time (the UTC + 0time zone) since 12:00 AM, January 1, 1970. This enables a single, commonly interpretable, floating point number to represent any date and time. The only drawback is that for a human reader it is not intuitive. The timestamp) (and fromtimestamp) (features enable our human-interpretable datetime object to be converted to and from an UNIX epoch for computational convenience.

4. Weekday ()

Sets the day of the week for a particular date.

#Monday is 0, Sunday is 6 weekday number= start datetime.date)(.weekday) (the fourth trick in our bag is the weekday) (function. It calculates the day of the week for any specified date. To use it, call on your datetime the date () function. This isolates the item from the date and ignores the part of time. And then call the feature of her weekday). This returns an amount from 0 to 6, where Monday is zero, Tuesday is one, and Sunday is six. It handles all the quirks of keeping track of the week's days so you don't need it.

5. Date strings

#Pass a date string and an interpretation code.

New datetime= datetime.datetime.strptime('2018-06-21,' percent Y-percent m-percent d')

#Turn a datetime into a date string.

Datestr= new datetime.strftime('percent Y-percent m-percent d') print(datestr) >>>' 2018-06-21'

Finally, we come to trick number five, which converts a date to and from a string. This is especially useful when we ingest data from a text file and want to convert text dates into datetime objects. It's also useful if we want to reveal or export our datetime item to a user in a text file.

To do this, we use the functions strptime) (and strftime). We need to provide a string specifying the format when making a conversion in either direction. percent Y' is the year in this code snippet,' percent m' is the month of two digits, and' percent d' is the day of two digits.

In fact, as a side note, there is one correct way in dates to represent years, months and days:' YYYY-MM-DD.' (An global standard, ISO 8601, was developed in 1988.) For instance, in this format, it would be' 2018-07-31' on 31 July 2018. I highly recommend that you format your dates so that you can be easily interpreted and compatible whenever you choose. Be warned, though, that in the wild there are a multitude of date formats. Be ready to make some twisted conversions to get all the information you ingest into that format.

You're now equipped with the five most helpful datetime tricks.

Combine timedelta, time stamp, weekday) (and string formatting to and from time stamps.

With these in your toolbox, you are 90% of the way in your next python project to solve all the date and time challenges.

EXERCISE

Write down the main programs in the examples, using the statements of conditions: if statement, for example, loop through an iterable loop through a sequence of numbers while loop break continues

List and demonstrate how to use the 5 tricks in python

Conclusion

Learning how to get started with computer programming may seem like a large challenge. You can go with many distinct programming alternatives, but many of them are difficult to learn, will take some time to figure out, and will not always do all the things you need. Many people are afraid they need to be smart or have a lot of education and coding experience before they can make it to the level of coding they want. But, even a beginner may get into programming with Python.

Whether you're a beginner or have been in this field for some time, Python has made it so easy to code. The language is English-based, so it's simple to read, and it's got rid of many of the other symbols that make coding difficult for others to read. And since it's a user domain, to make things easier, as anyone can make changes and see other codes.

This guidebook has discussed the distinct tasks you can do in Python for some time and how simple it is to get started for a beginner. You will find this process is easy and with a little practice, you can learn it and be extremely good at it. It's simple to use, it operates across a lot of platforms, and even the newest Mac devices come with it downloaded already.

Be sure to check out Python when you're prepared to start programming, or you want to discover a program that will do a lot of great things without all the hassle. This is one of the most popular programming options, and you'll find it easy to read and learn, even if you don't know how to get started first.

Hopefully, this book assisted you on your journey to become a computer programmer or stroked the passion for learning to program. If you mastered the ideas in this text, interesting and helpful programs are being written just for you. The basic concepts of computer science and software engineering should also be firmly founded. I can only say "go for it" if you are interested in studying these fields in greater depth. Maybe one day you'll also consider yourself a computer scientist. I'd be delighted if the eBook played a very small part of that process.